THE *CHURCH* MADE FLESH

Other titles by Alan Todd

The Question
The Audacity to Believe – A 10-day devotional
The Audacity to Believe – Workbook

THE *CHURCH* MADE FLESH

Regaining Foundational Principles and
Practices of the Apostolic Church

ALAN TODD

THE CHURCH MADE FLESH
REGAINING FOUNDATIONAL PRINCIPLES AND PRACTICES OF THE APOSTOLIC CHURCH

iUniverse books may be ordered through booksellers or by contacting:

iUniverse
1663 Liberty Drive
Bloomington, IN 47403
www.iuniverse.com
1-800-Authors (1-800-288-4677)

ISBN: 978-1-4917-4154-2 (sc)
ISBN: 978-1-4917-4156-6 (hc)
ISBN: 978-1-4917-4155-9 (e)

Print information available on the last page.

iUniverse rev. date: 06/03/2015

Dedicated

I dedicate this book to my family, who has inspired me to be everything that God has intended. The countless hours I was away writing, traveling, and counseling, I was always excited to come home.

To church leaders, young and old men, and women who desire to be change agents before the return of our Lord.

Contents

Acknowledgments

Writing a book is a great undertaking that consumes many hours and much energy. The satisfaction and joy however is very rewarding. This book would not be possible if it had not been for a great number of people who have come along side to assist in its completion. My editorial team, Shirleen Weekes, Kristy Salmon, Matthew Longmore, Elliott Thompson, Dinah Whitton and Paul Thomas have contributed greatly to the formulation of the original manuscript. Their keen and watchful eyes caught much of my rambling and slovenliness. When I was uncertain about particular sections, they guided me and encouraged me to stick to the main thoughts and ideas. With their insights, they encouraged me to make the text a more readable document, one that would accomplish the original intent. For this, I am grateful.

To my pastors, Bishop D.W. Thompson and Mother E. Thompson and the entire Bethlehem United Church organization for the opportunity they have given me over the years to serve the body of Christ. Without their care and guidance, I would not have been able to have any content for this book. To the late F.W. McKenzie, who was never my pastor directly, but took the time to mentor me in our many one on one sessions to talk about what it takes to grow in the ministry. To Bishop S. A. Dunn, the great apostle of our time, who forged ahead amidst tremendous adversity and planted churches, sent out workers, my pastor being one, and has left a great Apostolic heritage and legacy. To the local church, I have had the honour of serving these past few years, Global Apostolic Ministries; you have been the testing ground, the pruning hook by which God cut me, making me ready for greater service in the Kingdom. Last but not least, my family; Allison, my wife, added her incredible editorial corrections and comments and has supported me through this entire process. She has been my greatest supporter. There were moments that the text sat as I contemplated abandoning the project but Allison encouraged me to complete it. For this, I am thankful. She is a great life partner.

List of Illustrations

Foreword

When Alan approached me to write a foreword to this remarkable book, I was genuinely humbled that he should bestow such honor upon me. As I started reading the manuscript, I was strongly impressed. Here was what I felt deep in my heart being expressed in a manner that was beyond my ability to express. Was this coincidental? I thought not.

For a while now I have expressed the conviction that unless we, the members of the Apostolic Church, are prepared to sacrifice ourselves, spend and be spent for the Kingdom, we will never see the move of God that so many of us dream about. I am convinced, that as long as we are content to render service that is merely convenient, as long as we continue to be satisfied with the mediocre, as long as we are satisfied with merely "having church", as long as we, insanely, continue to do the same things in the same way, while expecting different results, the apostolic revival that we hope for *"will remain but a fleeting illusion to be pursued but never attained."*

The world has changed more in the last ten years than it did in the previous one hundred years. Yet we in the apostolic movement appear to be blissfully unaware of this and continue to chug along at horse and buggy speed trying desperately to play catch up with the kingdom of darkness. We have taken too much for granted for too long. I fear that we are losing our relevance and thus, our influence. We cannot afford for this to happen. There is too much at stake. It is time for the Church of Jesus Christ to forsake the role of a thermometer, merely recording the temperature of the times and resume the role of a thermostat, determining the temperature of the times. We desperately need a paradigm shift. The question is: "How are we to make the transition? How are we to ensure that we advance the agenda of the Church and not our own? How is the Church of the Lord Jesus Christ to make itself relevant again? How will we effectively "serve this present age"?

I make bold to claim that the book that you now hold in your hands provides the answers. It is a seminal work, which will challenge, inspire, and change you. It demands, that we look at what Henry Drummond called "The Programme of Christianity", not through the lens of traditional apostolic culture, but through the lens of the biblical call of Jesus Christ on the life of every born-again child of God and the spirit and methods of the apostles, all in the context of the postmodern world in which we live. He examines how colonialism has affected the efforts of the Church to fulfill the Great Commission, exploring in the process, liberation theology, and white privilege. Particularly fascinating to me is the concept of "incarnationalism" espoused by Pastor Todd. It is his conviction that the people of God must enter into the experience of our Lord, becoming acquainted, as He did, with the world of the lost and loving them into a relationship with Him. In order to effectively accomplish this, we must be willing to pay the price of servanthood and death.

The whole book is full of concepts, which I would have dared to call "revolutionary" were it not for the fact that they are grounded in basic biblical principles, which, sadly have been either neglected or deliberately forsaken. Pastor Todd is so convinced himself of the efficacy of these principles that he has moved to institute them in the assembly, which he pastors.

If you are satisfied with the average, the mediocre, the "same old, same old" then this book will be too radical for you, but if you have enlisted in "the army of the dissatisfied", if you have come to the conclusion that no one should be thirsty where an abundance of water is present, if, like me, you long for a genuine and sustained move of God, then this book is a must read. Sir Francis Bacon, the English philosopher and author made the following observation:

> Some books are to be tasted, others to be swallowed, and some few to be chewed and digested: that is, some books are to be read only in parts, others to be read, but not curiously, and some few to be read wholly, and with diligence and attention (Bacon, 2007)

This is a book to be chewed and digested; it is to be read wholly with diligence and attention. I guarantee that if this course is followed, your concept of Christ and His Church will be radically altered. It will be a life changing experience.

I count Alan, his wife Allison, and their eight children as my friends. May the omnipotent, omniscient, omnipresent, immutable God bless them abundantly and use this book to assist in the transformation of His people globally.

John-Mark Bartlett
Pastor of Pentecostal Tabernacle
Kingston, Jamaica

Praise for *The Church Made Flesh*

I met Elder Alan Todd at a conference in Miami, Florida. What a treat! Let's come to terms with it: most of us need help. We could use a friend to assist when we deal with difficult subjects. Elder Alan Todd asked me to peruse sections of a book that needed to be written a long time ago. The read was so exciting that I was still reading at 2:00 a.m. It's powerful! Here is the subject: Galatians 3:26-29. Sit down with a cup of Jamaican Blue Mountain coffee and read this scripture. Take another cup and read it again.

Elder Todd then starts to fire very uncomfortable questions: Why do the black Churches stay black? Why do the white churches stay white? These are probing and incisive questions and yes, they need proper answers. Give yourself this book and then help God solve the next vexing problem in the North American Apostolic church. Sorry - this book is not designed to grace the shelf of your library. You should really read it on your knees. Embark on your journey with tears in your eyes.

Bishop Paul Reynolds
International Honorary General Presbyter
United Pentecostal Church International

I have had the singular privilege of ministering in the Church Alan serves in Toronto, Canada. During my short stay there, I have been impressed by the level of spirituality palpable in every aspect of his ministry. In him I detected a burden that recognizes and grapples with the modern challenges of multiculturalism, the forces that challenge the integrity of family life and an engagement in the world mission field, to name a few. Clearly, he is one of those rare leaders who cast a wide net in a perennial quest for giving, in the words of Oswald Chambers, *His Utmost For His Highest*. I have no doubt as to his credentials for writing this book. In fact, ministers of his caliber and burden can do no other than to share their Christ-distilled wisdom and experience with the body at large.

In this book, Alan takes the spiritual pulse of the Pentecostal/Apostolic Church and lays bare its true condition. Tapping into a rich spiritual repertoire of experiences, both anecdotal and other erudite sources, this book is a *tour de force* that revisits bedrock issues such as the cost of discipleship, church-planting and church order, among others. Employing a fruitful dialectic of tension, these issues are explored in the intersection between the nascent Apostolic Church of the first century AD and its contemporary incarnation. The denouement is an incisive, accessible, candid, and profound exposition that is a must in every discerning minister and layperson's library.

Paul Thomas, PhD
(Education, King's College, London)
Lecturer, University of Oslo, Norway
Institute for Pedagogy
Comparative and International Education
Superintendent of the Apostolic Church
International Fellowship, Europe

Pastor Todd's work is a heart's cry for us to return back to do the work God called us to - soul winning. He presents a lucid, scholarly, and sometimes uncomfortably challenging argument that stirred the spirit of evangelism deep within... Read it, and then go to the work you were called to do!

Nicholas Myers
Elder, Bethel United Church of
Jesus Christ Apostolic (Camberwell),
London England.

As one who is deeply involved in the ministry of Evangelism within my local church, I have found *The Church Made Flesh* the heartbeat of God for the church and is truly Apostolic in its nature. Alan has compiled a great work meant to be embedded in our hearts and not just our bookcases. I recommend every Pastor and lay leader read this to help set a fresh vision for their ministry. This is a wonderful ministry tool.

Dean Delpeache,
Director, Evangelism & Community Outreach,
APC Pickering

The Church Made Flesh challenges today's commonly adopted church system of attraction by comparing the 1st century church model, which exercises apostolic authority by going out into the world. Without apology Alan combats the readers thinking on how well today's church is executing the Great Commission and touching the lives of people of all nations. For those that are ready to effect change in this world the biblical way, this is a book that you must not only have but study and wrestle with.

Michael Whitton,
Minister of Operations, Global Apostolic Ministries
Toronto, Canada

Introduction

All life forms come into being by some birthing process. They grow, mature, and die. At each stage, vital developments take place, which give the life form its characteristics and uniqueness. It is foolish to believe that any life form is static and will not change, evolve, develop and decay. I am amazed by the simple wonder of humanity. I see a small baby and the thought strikes me that, one day, that baby will be a grown person. Conversely, I look at a mother or some other aged person and I am baffled at the thought that she was once a small child. Now this is such a normal reality for us, that we seldom, if ever, really think about how marvelous it is. We never see a person grow, yet we see them grow. My wife and I have brought home eight babies. They are all different, but through the process of growth, they become grown people. There was not a day when I saw them literally stretch and grow physically, but day by day, they got taller, heavier and more intelligent.

Living things don't stay the same. So it is with the church. She is an organism, a living entity, made up of living parts required to carry out distinct duties and service. The size of the body doesn't impact how critical and important it is for each component to function optimally; it is a living system, therefore, all elements of its organization are necessary for its survival, irrespective of the organizations' size; big or small all the systems must work in an exacting, complex way that contributes to growth.

Change is obviously important in any organizational system. The intention of this book, however, is not merely to present a prescription for needed change, but rather to explore what requirements are needed for useful change, and why. Unfortunately, some people are threatened by the discussion of change; however, my goal is to look at some of the critical elements of needed change. Emphasis will be laid on regaining a strong missional drive for the church, and it will be impossible to address this issue without talking about how we have arrived at our present state of affairs. I will share some of my personal experiences, which are not to be read as objective realities for everyone, but subjective experiences, which I have confronted. Many of you will have your own experience and I welcome you to blend them into what you read. What I am referring to specifically is how we have taken practices of *the church*, (principles of the first century Apostolic church), amalgamated those principles into a Roman church system and made it compatible with the original design[1]. For years I never seriously questioned the elements of *"how we do church"* (how we practice our faith), thinking it to be divine practice, that our liturgical practice is a biblical and authoritative system not to be deviated from. What made this worse for me was that I had studied theology and religion in Bible College, worked in my local church in various capacities, worked in para-church organizations, pastored a congregation from near dissolution through to revitalization and never stopped to think deeply about how we were doing the work of the ministry. The rare occasion I did stop to consider our task, I quickly dismissed it or tried to adapt some new fashionable whim that would be the answer to the church's growth problems. I think that the dismissal was really an inability to maneuver my way out of the seventeen-century-long structures. These structures were so ingrained and embedded in our practice that it seemed almost sacrilegious to try to change or question it.

I remember the time I began experimenting with some novel forms of worship in the early years of my pastoral ministry. We were encountering many people coming to our church who had never been exposed to church practice and culture, the "unchurched" as we call them. In the spirit of faithfulness to organizational practice, I buckled down, thinking that doing things the way they had always been done would suffice. Big mistake! After several months of this, I realized that new members and visitors where having a very difficult time assimilating to our cultural attitudes and practices about worship; numbers began to decline, suggesting that to effectively assimilate and acculturate these people into the fellowship, we needed to do things differently. I remember clearly being instructed that all

---

[1] Maybe the issue isn't really that we have taken those ancient principles and adapted them into a new church system, as much as we have blindly continued to perpetuate a system we inherited, never asking questions as to why this has happened and how it has impacted the church's ability to stay true to her calling.

worship practices were to be kept the same, because all the churches in the organization locally, as well as internationally, were practicing church in the same way. The idea behind this thinking was that anyone from any of our churches could visit from any place in the world and fall right into place. It was no doubt a franchising of the ministry, a sort of "McDonaldization"[2] of the church, suggesting that all the churches in a particular network of churches are expected to function within the same mode of ministry and liturgy. George Ritzer, who coined this nominalization, defines it as:

> The process by which the principles of the fast-food restaurant are coming to dominate more and more sectors of American society as well as the rest of the world...McDonaldization has shown every sign of being an inexorable process, sweeping through seemingly impervious institutions (e.g., religion) and regions of the world (e.g., European nations such as France) (Ritzer 1993,2013, 1).

If you have ever visited a McDonald's restaurant anywhere in the world, you will notice the duplication of business practice, with the exception of some local menu items. This is not a bad thing necessarily; however, we have no basis for this kind of practice in the church of Jesus Christ. There was this prevailing idea that, in order for the church to be successful, it had to follow the same model of other more established churches[3], primarily, the headquarter church. This attitude completely ignored the extreme cultural polarization of each church in its different context. It made little difference that we were dealing with third generation Canadians who had little familiarity, at best, with hymns, and found the Kings James Bible very difficult to read. Not to mention the aspect of our worship experience that was born out of a deep Caribbean attitude. I wasn't advocating the sole

---

[2]   This term is a synthesized rendering of a business term which speaks of the church duplicating the idea of a business franchise

[3]   I use the term "established" to refer to churches that have achieved a level of organizational maturity, where they have moved out of being an infant start up ministry and more able to operate independent of any other group.

use of contemporary songs or for a different translation of the Bible (mind you toning down the strong reggae rhythm wouldn't have hurt). Rather, I was recommending that our practice should be far more adaptable to the uniqueness of a church's immediate cultural context. At that time, unfortunately, I decided to conform to the conventional practice, at least temporarily, until I was more confident that the amendments I was considering would actually facilitate genuine growth.

While at Bible College, I had specialized in Religious History and for some reason, I could not stop questioning how we were "doing" church in our era. Were we using principles and practices that ordained by God for the maximum effect on the world or, were we using man made systems that seemed to fit into our compulsion to control the ministry? How did I manage to miss the subtlety of churchmen in the post-apostolic era, and the baseness of the cold and frigid attitude of the mid and dark ages? In addition, how did I miss the valiant, but weak, attempt to regain the lost New Testament model for explosive growth in the Kingdom of God during the Reformation?

Over the past few years, I have realized that I am among a growing group of believers and leaders that are tired of the dry and never-changing traditional church practice. I am also weary of pursuing the hottest church growth trends that seemed to pop up in our popular Christian culture. I believe that somehow, somewhere, there is a move of God lingering, waiting for the few brave, un-intimidated, adventurous people who are hungry for nothing less than a pulsating move of God.

In this book, I want to engage not just those who are in leadership; the issues of the church must be understood by every believer. While we understand that leadership has a particular role to play in the shaping of the church and its practice, they are not the only ones who should explore critical issues of the church. Our culture seems to be enamored by the cult of leadership[4], thinking that unless we bow at its altar, we can never understand what is necessary for the faith community to progress.

This reading is not for the faint at heart. I will challenge many assumptions about ministry that are held as sacred, infallible and divine. These are simply

---

[4] This phrase refers to the idea that we have become a culture that is fixated on leadership; and as important as leadership is in the church, it has aided the divide between those who serve in frontline ministry and those who sit in the pews.

practices and traditions that we employ as a means of expressing our faith toward God. Unfortunately, we are now faced with the fact that our current church practices have become so entrenched, and we haven't notice that we have lost ground, becoming very extraneous in a world that needs us to be relevant. Do not take this warning for granted. If you do, it will reveal itself in several ways. Some of you will read and intellectually agree with me, but resolve that it is not practical or possible to do anything about it. Others will defend the present structures, and may find scriptures to validate that the things done, are the way God wants them to be done, therefore insinuate that I am trying to change things God does not want changed. Then there is the group who, upon reading, will be provoked to do their own research to find out who else is feeling this way; they will go through their Bibles and begin leafing through its pages to re-examine the practice of the early church. And still there is a group that may take it further and begin studying the church in its historical context, at least the first three to four centuries, to see what took place and how it has impacted our present age. Whichever category you find yourself, I solicit your indulgence to read this book to its completion.

I have found that, to a great extent, not only are the doctrines of the church inspired, but the practices as well. The Apostles were not only given a divinely inspired message, but they were also given a divinely inspired practice. Acts 2:42 gives us a glimpse of this;

*"They devoted themselves to the apostles' **teaching** and to **fellowship**, to the **breaking of bread** and to **prayer**"* [emphasis mine]

I am not trying to be provocative to the point that I discredit any achievements of the church. I believe that this enquiry is a passionate pursuit for the faith which was once delivered unto the saints and must be contended for at all cost. Leonard Sweet, states, "...nothing fails like success...", I must admit, the systems and practices that we have used, worked fairly well in past years, but these same practices are failing tremendously, within our changing cultural ethos, to meet the challenges of shifting tides in a post-Christian world.

This book is written to draw attention to some of the fundamental processes that have driven our current attitude towards the mission of the church and its operational development. Consequently, I lay a foundation in this volume with the intention to invite you to digest the concepts presented and prepare you to wrestle with these ideas, which I believe are necessary adjustments for ministry in the end time. My focus here is to encourage you to think about what the church should be and how she should be acting in order to see revival in this age. The kind of revival I am advocating is not the kind that most church-going people have become accustomed to -the idea that we can schedule a revival on a particular weekend. Rather, I am advocating a revival of sinners coming into closer proximity with the life changing power of Jesus, manifested through the lives of ordinary, transformed people who themselves have been resuscitated by the power of the Holy Spirit. This means the church could very well look much different than what we are familiar with. This revival may birth movements not structured after the mega church model that seems to enchant many new leaders and churches today. Maybe we will see smaller groups of people assembled for worship but interconnected with a network of believers in many places. I used the word "maybe", because I don't want to imply that the Holy Spirit has only one way that He works among people. This is another area where we often make a mistake; we think that the way we do things, is the only way to do it. Stop and ask yourself, is the way we do things divinely inspired or are we perpetuating old systems and practices? Is there a possibility that there is a better way?[5]

---

[5] Many pastors with an older mindset believe they were not called to change things, but instead to uphold what was given. I agree that the fundamental doctrines and principles must be upheld and contended for; at the same time, change is essential to progress and growth. Knowing what to change and what not to change is the critical issue. Let me give an example of how to know what and when change is necessary. Years ago, we used to dedicate babies on the first Sunday of each month. I can't recall what prompted the research into the origins of the practice but we found out that the first Sunday practice in our fellowship came out of necessity. Our presiding Bishop used the first Sunday to dedicate babies as a logistical necessity. Many of the branch Churches that were recently started came together on the first Sunday, so naturally a convenient time to dedicate the babies from the smaller churches. It was and remains a good practice, but it is not a divine ordinance to shackle us. Our ministry coordinates baby dedications as the need arises.

In Section I, we will focus on the structure Jesus introduced in th, building of the church. He said "upon this Rock I will build my church…". There is no indication that that process has stopped, the fact that Jesus has not returned means He is still building His church. According to Peter, the building materials are people. How the structure is built is the question of our inquiry. It is very likely there may be practices in the process not yet revealed to us. My effort is to provoke your thinking about what Jesus has been doing; how He has been with us; as well as His expectations of us as fellow-workers in the kingdom. We will examine the call of Jesus upon those who desire be His disciples. Our modern church world seems void of the tenacity that the early disciples possessed. Commitment, a difficult quality to find in the body of Christ today, remains the stamp of all spiritual graces in working for the Lord. Many have been deluded to believe that we are living in some kind of utopic world that offers us the luxuries of all the creature comforts our hearts desire. Therefore, even though we have come into faith with Christ, we have a very shallow display of hazardous living; something of which the early church had no shortage.

We could break down church ministry essentially into two types: those who transfer the Gospel with its life changing power into every member of that congregation, and those who merely captivate people with entertainment and showmanship. I will demonstrate how the first type of church gets more done for God, than the self-consumed, entertainment driven ones will. To close the section we will take a special look at the lives of three New Testament giants: builders and layers of the foundation of the Church, Paul, Peter and James and their roles in the development of the early church. There is no doubt we have moved ahead in time and technology, but given to these men was the genius for laying the ground work for the greatest enterprise, the greatest organization, the earth has ever known – The Church of Jesus Christ.

In Section II, we will examine what is the most significant aspect of this book - *Incarnationalism*. This is the missing link in 21st century apostolic ministry. I want to present to you the way I believe we should be thinking about how we practice faith in a congregational capacity. What I present may prove intellectually difficult and even practically impossible. Nevertheless, I come with a fair amount of conviction that this will put us on the right track. What is the incarnation? How does it influence our philosophy of ministry? Moreover, what does it look like in operation? These and other crucial questions are addressed in this section. There are dimensions of the churches vitality that I do not address, not because I do not think them important but rather they fall outside of the scope of this book. It is the role of spiritual disciplines to impact culture; for example the role of prayer that precedes revival, fasting and sensitivity to God, unity of the saints, and ardent and powerful preaching. These, coupled with what we present here, are the critical essentials for a powerful end-time great commission church.

In Section III, we will examine how a large population of churches have operated from a destructive and dysfunctional psychological framework that has fundamentally annulled the execution of their missional responsibility; it is the plight of oppressed people in the execution of the Great Commission. We cannot honestly deal with the lack of missional vitality in these churches without first understanding some of the fundamental handicaps that have hindered the work of God. I want to stimulate a powerful missional movement from oppressed "Centre's" that will be the catalysis for what I believe will be a great end-time revival worldwide. If God used oppressed people in times past, I think we should look closely on the horizon for the next move of the Spirit, for a rebirth of a passion for God in people and the desire to see others transformed by the same power.

In the final section, chapters 11 and 12, we will take a journey into the great question of an Apostolic inheritance. I am convinced that we have lost the fire that the early apostles felt. I think we have lost the kingdom vision for an expansive church. Instead, we are concerned in mini-empire building. This wouldn't be so bad if we were motivated by a vision to see souls saved all over the world; but when we fight territorially over a very limited space, which we believe is "mine", in this vast planet, we cease to be a force to contend with. If every Apostolic pastor and church had a vision for planting more churches in the earth, we would see a greater move of God and much more people would realize the Kingdom of God.

Largely, what I am addressing in this book is the church's business of church planting; it is about people thinking differently about their role in the ministry. Furthermore, it is about current church leaders (pastors and others) rethinking the role they play in mobilizing the saints for the work of the ministry. My desire is to break down walls that we have erected so we can have a clearer vision of the future of the church I believe God wants. I do not know the total mind of God, I share with you what I believe the Lord has inspired me to share; I pray that I will provoke you to a transformation in your thinking and that you will be motivated to do some things differently.

You may ask, why do we have to consider doing things differently? The answer may not be readily apparent, but allow me to share with you some of the social developments that have not only impacted our world, but has altered what we as Christians must face in the business of ministry. Secular humanism and a materialistic worldview have assumed control of the major institutions in the Western world. The Christian worldview and influence has dissipated. Let me interject; I am not of the belief that the Christian faith will disappear completely – at the end of time we win. But, this does not mitigate the ferocity of the satanic battle that rages in this age. On one hand, we face the battle that rages *within* our church walls, which is casting serious doubts as to the impact of our work. Kevin Swanson, in a riveting book, *Apostate: The Men who Destroyed the Christian West*, writes, "Many churches can hardly be bothered by the fact that the last twenty years of ministry have produced a 97% apostasy rate among the twenty-somethings!"[6] We have lost a chunk of young people, and along with this, we must contend with what is happening *without* the walls of the church. There has been a steady and rapid decline of moral purity; for example, those knighted with the honour of instructing young people in University and College play a huge role in this dissension. A recent report in the Washington Post chronicled that "Religious services take a back seat for many faculty members, with 51 percent saying they rarely or never attend church or synagogue and 31 percent calling themselves regular

---

[6] Swanson, K., *Apostate: The Men who Destroyed the Christian West.* Colorado, Generations with Vision, 2013

churchgoers". Of the "professors and instructors surveyed (over 1600 from over 180 institutions) they are, strongly or somewhat, in favor of abortion rights (84 percent); and believe homosexuality is acceptable (67 percent)"[7]. Taking an aerial view, a survey of the last five decades gives us a sampling of the contributing factors of our moral and cultural decline: Rock music, drugs and rebellion came in the 1960's and 70's, the dating culture in the 1950's – 60's, the shacking up culture of the 1970's- 90's, Eminem's 'rape rap' of the 2000's, fatherlessness of the 1980's into the 2020', the hook-up culture of the 2000's – 2020's, the huge rise in homosexuality 1980's -2020's, the abortion culture – over 100 million babies killed since 1960's into 2020's, and as it stands now, we are looking at some 80 million elderly soon to be euthanized.

In the words of a ministerial colleague, Pastor A. Castro, *we must play the hand we are dealt.* Therefore, the harvest field is ripe. The old fashion sickle, however, may not be adequate for the harvest before us. When I suggest doing things different, I am alluding to the massive work that only a great commission focused believer and ministry can contemplate. This kind of church is willing and ready to face the challenges before us, head on.

Alan Todd,
Global Apostolic Ministries
Toronto, Canada

---

[7] http://www.washingtonpost.com/wp-dyn/articles/A8427-2005Mar28.html

A Word on *Emergence*

There has been some debate as to the usage of the term *emergence* among some Pentecostal and Evangelical groups. I do not wish to join that debate, but felt it important to at least give a brief explanation for how I understand and use the term. I assume much of the debate rises from the quarters of Christendom that have accepted the present methods of operations as normative and even authoritative. I found that the Emergence Movement calls into question two things. One, the way we practice church and secondly, some emergence groups even question the absoluteness of truth; calling into question God and the Bible as the sources of truth. The proposition in this book is that the church has moved very far from the first century model given by the Lord to His apostles as to the practices of the Church. In order to return to a former operation with the propensity for revival, an emergent spirit is required, something not seen for some 17 centuries. Emergent thinking calls many practices into question, desires a new way of "doing" things and seeks to make the Gospel an impacting force beyond current church and Christian traditions. We are well aware that some traditions are hurtful and destructive but we also know that many traditions are critical for the continuation of the Gospel. Therefore, this is not an attack on fundamental Christian doctrine, on orthodoxy. I hope that you will be spiritually sensitive and discerning and not see this as an attack on the Church. What is at the root of this book is the desire to see the Church in the state of glory promised by the Lord, a revisiting of apostolic revival where the world can be turned upside down once again. Emergence in this context is to see the church rising out of the ashes of a static old system that is not elastic enough to move with the times, and challenging church practices that have morphed into a less than authentic apostolic entity. In the Book of Acts, people where saved on road sides while journeying home (Acts 8); some were baptized late in the night, not because they were hiding, but because that was when they made decisions to be saved (Acts 16). Compare that to the underlining belief now held by many, that conversion happens at or in a church building on Sunday mornings. What makes emergence so difficult is that we have made our traditions and practices sacred. An emergent spirit says there is no absolute truth to the "practice", the "expression" of faith. We can do things differently.! I don't mean to patronize, but do we read at the beginning of a service or the end? Do we stand or sit? I have actually heard serious debates, with scripture, on this topic and people have fought for a right and wrong position. Really? It doesn't matter! The key thing is that scripture is read

Finally, I am proposing, while we can do things differently, we hold to some fundamental apostolic truths. Acts 2:42 gives them to us; *apostolic teaching, fellowship, breaking bread, and prayers.* Paul further expands on this in his instructions to Timothy, *"Till I come, give attendance to reading, to exhortation, to doctrine"* (1 Timothy 4:13). These are fundamental Apostolic instructions; we cannot and should not deviate from them. "How" we do them is what an emergent thinker will question. The "how" is not sacred, but can be inspired.

SECTION I

Upon this Rock

> "...I will build my church..."
> *- Jesus*

Sitting in private conference with his band of emergent leaders, Jesus questions his team as to what the word on the street was about his identity. "What are people saying about me? Who do they say I am?" Each man begins to scan his memory to share the comments they had heard. One by one, they began to share. "Some people are saying that you are Elijah, the mighty prophet of renown; your characteristics and power remind them of his ministry. Some are saying that you are Jeremiah, the weeping prophet who foretold of the judgment on God's people", remarked one. "Well, I heard some people saying that you are Moses resurrected"; 'I heard some ladies saying you are Samuel". After hearing them, Jesus asks, "but who do you say I, the son of man, am?" The group is silent, now the attention is off others and has shifted to them. A wrong answer could potentially be detrimental to their leader's perception of them. No one dared to answer for fear; a wrong answer would show their inability to discern who he was, even after spending so much time with him. But it is at this point that one of the disciple ponders the question, hears a whisper from heaven, and, out of the silence boldly declares absolute truth:, *"Thou art the Christ, the Son of the living God"* - Cephas (Matt. 16:16). In that moment, eyes pierce back and forth between Jesus and Peter. Time had stood still. For in that instant a divine revelation is transmitted from heaven into the spirit of a man that would later deny that he ever knew Jesus.

The hymnologist, C. Bishop wrote, *"That God would love a sinner such as I..."* This very sentiment is true for Peter. God had downloaded to him the greatest revelation a man could receive. Jesus was God manifested in the flesh. He was the Lamb of God, the light of God, the bread of life, the peace of God. He was the fullness of the Godhead bodily, He was the entire Divine Being wrapped in a robe of flesh. This knowledge was so wonderful and magnificent it could not have come from the local schools of religion, philosophy, or science. This knowledge was so wonderful that mere man could not pass it on from generation to generation. It was a unique moment in time; God laid out the basic principle and truth upon which the entire church would be built, and interestingly, he chose to use a man like Peter to initiate the work.

With confident satisfaction, the Lord responded to Peter saying, *"You are Peter, and upon this 'rock' I will build My church and the gates of hell shall not prevail against it"*. Jesus said that He was going to build His church upon 'the rock' of revelation that Peter had uttered. The fundamental principle is that the church would be erected on a body of truth, and that truth was a person – Jesus Christ; not a man-made religious system, not human traditions and ceremonies, not in any disciple or teacher, not on any saint but entirely and exclusively on the person of Christ.

With eyes and ears attentive to His voice, Jesus begins to teach them the principles of truth that He would use to build the church. Peter would later teach that each disciple was a lively stone building up a spiritual house, in which the general contractor was Jesus (1 Peter 2:5). There is a dual aspect to this principle: first, that Jesus himself is the builder and second, that He is the thing on which the church is built. What is powerful about this, and carries some measure of mystery, is that He hands authority over to people, *"the called"* out people of God, to continue the building process. Whatever they would bind or loose on earth would be recognized in Heaven as such. In this, Jesus introduces and invites us into a shared work of the ministry. Since Jesus is building the church and He includes us in the process, it is prudent for us to examine how He started and whom He used. We must identify the qualities of the materials used and under what conditions He began to erect the structure.

Let's look at this a bit closer and from the vantage point of several key builders in the New Testament. I ask you to go deeper than surface reading or reading for information purposes only. Look into this with a keen eye and analyze for yourself elements of how we practice the building of the church today.

CHAPTER 1

Jesus, the Master Builder

Preparedness:

There are several things worthy of our consideration when we look at Jesus' building methods. These features should guide our practice of church work. The first is timing. We hear very little of Jesus' ministry until he is well into his adult life. He comes on the scene at age 30 and his ministry only lasted three years. There is a saying: "Success happens when preparedness meets opportunity and is seized". We should not focus, however, primarily on success; this has become one of the major priorities and motivations of our age. Success should have its rightful place in our lives, but it is preparedness that should consume us. The art of becoming, growing, learning, and evolving into the kind of creature God intends, should be our focus, and this process takes time. In a popular song sung by Miley Cyrus, *The Climb*,[8] this is impeccably captured. What should preoccupy our attention is the journey, the climb.

What should preoccupy our attention is the journey, the climb. Inundated with being successful, we fail to see that the process towards success is an enormous part of that success.

The writer of this song hit the nail on the head. Most of us seek the destination and try to side step the process. We want it quick, fast, and easy with as little pain as possible. Listen to success: *struggle, getting knocked down, facing mountains, voices of doubt and fear, feeling directionless* and, *uphill battles*. True victory, true success, comes from "the climb".

---

[8] http://www.elyrics.net/read/h/hannah-montana-lyrics/the-climb-lyrics.html

The rotation of the earth around the sun takes 365 days as a cycle; so it takes time for each of us to revolve around the "Son" until we become like Him. As the earth revolves around the sun, we experience seasons. Each season prepares us in different ways for the work that lies before us. Have you ever thought about those 30 years of silence in the life of Jesus? Some have said that Jesus traveled to the Orient to learn ancient teaching. I won't be so speculative since I haven't found any evidence that substantiates such a theory. I would rather think he was immersed in his culture. I believe he was living, sharing, participating in the everyday realities of Jewish life. I believe he was reading and studying Torah in the synagogue. To a great extent, our preparedness for the work of the church is deeply embedded in our willingness to immerse ourselves in the lives of the people we desire to reach and serve. In fact, this is one of the missiological practices of missionaries that enter the mission field. Often times the missionary must first spend a great deal of time in the host culture deciphering language, culture, customs, manners, etc. I remember when we began research & development work in the planting of a church in the Caribbean. We spent the first two years learning the distinctiveness of the culture, and the attitudes and customs of the people. We were careful not to assume anything because there was much North American influence. It would have been very easy for our team to think that we could just go, preach, and minister. That would have been a grave mistake. This is the wonderful teaching of incarnationalism often left out of our theology and philosophy of ministry. How willing are we to become like the people to whom we desire to minister? How willing are we to share in their pain, struggle, frustrations, poverty, sadness, loss, and brokenness in order to share the love, life, peace, and joy of the Lord?[9] When

---

[9]   At the time of the writing of this book, our church had commissioned a missionary to work in the Caribbean Island of St. Vincent. Our missionary is from the country of Zimbabwe. She had never heard of the Island at the time she accepted an invitation to pilgrim on a short-term trip. While on the field, the Lord spoke to her heart to give up everything and return immediately to work in this field. It is a year later and the novelty had worn off. The work is tough, requiring much prayer, patience, love, discipline and focus. She has laboured and contended with those who have little knowledge of walking with the Lord. In all this, she has incarnated herself in the life of the community and each day is a journey of becoming all things to all men that she may win some.

Jesus said, "come unto me..." (Matt. 11:28), he wasn't speaking as someone who didn't understand what it felt like to be over-taxed and to struggle with unfair political practices that hindered a normal and happy life. The potency inherent in his invitation resonated with his contemporaries because he had been baptized into the everyday struggles of his Jewish countrymen.

Although he was God in the flesh, he didn't rush to the cross. He settled into life with the people he came to save. In that process, he also had to face religious struggles in order to offer something different and better. Jesus took time with teachers, students, and fellow Jews, and experienced the struggles of a religious system that proved to be seriously empty of the power and authority of the presence of God. He lived through the highly religious practice of the Mosaic Law; it had become a hindrance to finding God instead of a path to him. Not that he didn't believe in it, or try to live it, he practiced it in its totality. He knew the essence of it, the element of it that brought life. Why? Because He was life. He made his life among the people, so he was able interpret the Word for what God really intended. The Scribes and Pharisees where preoccupied with keeping the letter of the Law, but their study of the Law missed one simple thing: it didn't invite them into the lives of the people they were being trained to teach. They became elite religious leaders who knew the Law better than everyone else, but not the spirit of the Law, and therefore lost the power to interpret the true meaning of the Law[10] to the people.

The incarnation has been a long lost doctrine in many, if not most Apostolic churches. Christendom has become more philosophical with theology that we have forgotten how to take theology and make it a reality in

---

[10] In my own life, God has used some extremely trying experiences to teach me that my life in a way is a shadow for what others experience. Sometimes as believers, we can become very insulated from the deep pain, fear, hurt and trauma of people around us. It is not until God humbles us and exposes us to the pain of others that we really begin to see the light of the glory of God. It is not until you have been sick unto death that we really feel what others feel. It is not until we have been charged falsely or not and suffer the malady of incarceration before we can feel the pain of seclusion. It is not until you lose a loved one (a child, a father, a mother) that you can really sit in the seat of persons who attend our churches and understand their pain. Somehow Jesus had this capacity. He felt what people felt and was able to minister to them.

our lives. Our theology has become a philosophical proposition, something we talk about but do not live to its fullest. The incarnation often preached or taught in the context of the Nativity narrative at Christmas time goes largely ignored. We have become believers that trivialize many *sacredly held beliefs*. Paul, the apostle, on the contrary, teaches something much different; his theological teaching is delivered as a response to the everyday circumstances of the believers. They are not philosophical propositions per se, but rather eternal, and some temporal truths, intended for application in practical situations. This is not pragmatism; it is more than that. It is weaving the eternal truths of scripture into the daily situations people encounter. Sometimes it calls for rebuke, chiding and even discipline; other occasions call for encouragement and yet others instructions. We have lost the basic elements of this great act of God coming into the world. The message is far more important than gift giving and special services at years end.

At its root, it is so deep that it should reflect the very essence of our ministries and church practice. What is the incarnation? The incarnation is the act of the great God humbling himself and taking on the form of a servant and becoming obedient unto death; this death was the death he suffered on the cross (Philippians 2). In order to do that, he had to come in *human form*. He must dress Himself in flesh, with all its affections, feelings, nerves, limitations, finality, and experience death. It is difficult to understand the trauma that Jesus must have experienced in the *Kenosis*[11]. Jesus is God, but for the act of becoming like us, like me, he must leave heaven dressed in this ridiculous garment called "flesh"; a spectacle to the heavenly host, a display of foolish limitation and depravity, and a sight of complete idiocy and total imprudence. That God, the eternal Spirit would bring Himself to such a low degree and be incarcerated in this lonely world; intimately surrounded first by his family and then 12 degenerate men, all deeply wounded and scared by their own human frailty, convicted sinners, guilty of all

---

[11] In Christian theology, kenosis (from the Greek word for emptiness κένωσις, kénōsis) is the 'self-emptying' of one's own will and becoming entirely receptive to God's divine will. The word ἐκένωσεν (ekénōsen) is used in Philippians 2:7, "[Jesus] made himself nothing ..." [Phil. 2:7] (NIV) or "...[he] emptied himself..." [Phil. 2:7] (NRSV), using the verb form κενόω (kenóō) "to empty".

manner of sins. Yet, He suffered the malady of their plight, willingly and obediently. It is not until we see him at Calvary that we witness the gravity and weight of this experience on him. Being in the flesh was torture, and an inscrutable and incomprehensible dilemma of Divine submission. I believe this is why he cries in the garden *"And now, Father, glorify thou me with thine own self with the glory I had with thee before the world was"* (John 17:5). Enough! This is enough! I can't bear this any longer! If you have never been restricted from something you hold dear to you, forced against your will and subjugated by powers beyond you, Jesus' experience may remain a mystery to you. Nevertheless, the time and task must be accomplished and death on the cross is the end of the road. Time must be served and not a minute longer or sooner. He yields, *"not my will, thine will be done"* (Luke 22:42). Without this likeness to humanity, the incarnation is not magnificent. Actually, our inability to perceive it, to understand it, may be a clue, as to why we struggle to serve the way we ought.

It is the fact that God became a man, which makes this His single most amazing act, ever. I can think of no other reason why He is my savior and my God. He surrendered everything to become like me, like us. The beauty of this revelation is that God drew near to me. It is this act of coming to me that has made me surrender myself; first to Him and then for the sake of others. However, I must confess I still struggle greatly with my inability to live up to that level of ministry.

I was speaking with a fellow brother the other day and he was wrestling with the incarnation. He struggled with the fact that Jesus, who is both God and man, came and dwelt among us. I said to myself, "Yes, this is the heart of the struggle, to be one thing – God, then to become like something else – man, with the sole intention to serve and save." We miss the full weight of what the incarnation really means for us. In a powerful and mysterious way, we are called into this fellowship of becoming like others in order to reach them. The absence of this genuine struggle is why our churches have become impotent, disconnected from the life of God and, invariably, the life of others. We don't know how to incarnate ourselves, like God did[12]. As simplistic as this may seem, I have always felt that the invitation to "follow me" is a serious call for each of us to walk the path He walked. Not just in the overt acts of goodness, but the messy acts of living, and being where people are. The more I study this topic, the more I feel so inadequate in my ability to serve. How much of me is willing to pour out myself, to be a living example of "kenosis" (to empty), emptying my inner man, my being, of desires and drives for the sake of others, and for the sake of Christ?. There is no question in my mind that the incarnation should be the thing that drives Apostolic ministry because it is the passion that compels us to serve. Somewhere the Apostolic church has lost this truth and, like many others, has become a church that preaches the incarnation, but is unwilling and unable to live it.

I will deal in more depth on the incarnation later. For now, let's just say that this act of God coming into the world is a major indication of what the Apostolic church and our ministries should embody. If we are serious and ready for revival, we must consider how He came. He came humbly, in a manger, not a palace. A great company of nobility did not surround the savior. His family, and some animals, wise men and an angelic host surrounded him. Compare His first advent with our lavish, pomp expressions, conferences, convocations, solemn assemblies, board meetings, programs and activities. None of these are inherently bad, many are actually necessary; the challenge is what we have made these events mean to us. We have become disconnected from the place real outreach ministry happens- not in these major church events, but in the arena where real people live. Denominations that focus on a social justice application to the work of the Gospel have done a much better job in this area than most mainline churches. The incarnation studied and applied to our individual

---

[12] Somewhere we have lost the capacity to give ourselves away. The church in this modern era is dangerously intoxicated with the wine of worldliness and self-centeredness. We want to be served (the word each week) but we are not serving – reaching the lost and strengthening the weak, encouraging other believers. I see deadness in many 21st century churches. Fornication has become the leading sin in the church. Not the sin of physical immorality, but the sort spoken of in Rev. 17. The world is drunk with the wine of fornication of the Women riding on the Beast. There is an immoral union between the spirit of the world and the spirit of the believers.

response and reaction to service is important; but it is in its collective application that we will see the greatest significance. Let us take some time and look at some fundamental elements of the design of the collective opportunities that are essential for a missional ministry focus. First, let's look at the role of teams.

Building Teams

One of Jesus' primary principles for building his church was the formulation and development of teams. It is impossible to think that there is such a thing called success without the aid of others. There is not a venture that man engages himself, where he can succeed alone. Even in solo sport events such as tennis, golf, and downhill skiing, a great collaboration of coaches and supporters makes success possible. The Master cultivated three levels of teams and it is important that we understand them to be affective at the "business" of ministry. He cultivated these teams in what I am calling the best places in the world: they are *the home, heaven* and, finally, *the ministry.* The work of the church and ministry cannot negate any of these teams. A careful examination of the New Testament reveals that Paul the Apostle, urged, first of all, that leaders in the church ensure they were cognizant of the value of relationships, primarily in their *homes* (1 Tim. 3:2 – 5; 11-13). This arena of relationship greatly affects the level of success achieved in the church.

The Best Place in the World: *The Home Team*

Jesus was no less focused in this area of life. It was important in Hebrew culture that family be the center of the well-being of children[13]. Jesus lived fully immersed in his culture. Mel Gibson, in one scene from his masterful portrayal of Jesus' last day in the *Passion of the Christ,* shows where Jesus' thoughts catapulted back in time to a memory of himself relating with his mother as a grown man. It depicts a side of Jesus with which we

---

[13] See the shema (Deut 6:4), the basic and fundamental instruction of home life, particularly the raising of children.

are unfamiliar. He is laughing, playing tricks, and enjoying time with his mother. The fall from a stool then brings us back into the reality of his Via Dolorosa journey to Calvary. We see their eyes piercing into each other's and we cannot hold back the tears, because we empathize with what it must feel like for a mother to see her son in that predicament, and with a son for his mother.

The weight of a Hebrew rabbi's authority largely depended on his family relationships. Matthew and Luke bring this to light as one listed a genealogy to showcase Jesus' royal roots, and the other to show his spiritual roots. Both show a different side of Jesus' family lineage. The point is, in the rabbi's tenure, it was significant for him to have a good family lineage. The continuity of faith was latent in the fabric of the family structure. If there was going to be a long-term missional existence, the message would need to be transmitted, not just in proselytizing the unconverted, but also, through a rich familial procession through multiple generations. We see this depicted in two biblical dramas. First, in Genesis 18:16-19, a striking statement is made to Abraham, indicating how important the continuity of the Gospel is to the Lord. The Lord and two angels visited Abraham; after pronouncing that Sarah would have a child, while He prepares to depart for Sodom, the Lord deliberates with the angels if He should share with Abraham His intentions on the wicked city. The reason the Lord gave for His disclosure to Abraham is one of the greatest revelations about how God feels and thinks about children and home life. The Lord said, "…For I know him [speaking of Abraham], that he will *command his children* and his household after him, and *they shall keep the way of the Lord*, to do justice and judgment…" If there was any reservation in the mind of the Lord concerning Abraham's ability to pass on the promise and the accompanying integrity, Abraham would not have been chosen.

The second account where the importance of family life is evident is the story of Israel in Egypt. It is at the tail end of their sojourn in Egypt that Moses comes on the scene. How does Moses come into the consciousness of who he really is? Demille, in the cinematic classic *The Ten Commandments*, portrays Jochebed, Moses' mother, releasing the infant Moses in a straw floating basket with a Levitical blanket wrapped around the child. The untrained eye may miss the point, but the inference is that he would one day realize where he really came from, the tribe of Levi, an

Isrealite. Nepheterie, the sister of the Pharaoh, in a desperate attempt to save the child and claim him as hers, sinks the basket but keeps the blanket, a mistake on her part but a divine providence, on God's. It is years later, this blanket becomes the trigger that sends Moses on a journey into his familial heritage. I believe the story line may speak to fundamental truths in the Hebrew culture.

One of the sad realities today is that for many ministries and Christian workers, service is overwhelming the call to the home team, the family. Pastors, musicians and all kinds of church leaders and workers have walked out on their families while continuing to serve in ministry. Divorce is swiftly becoming a standard practice in the church and among Christian ministers. On national television, pastors announce their divorces to audiences as if it were some virtuous act of piety. Pastors confess to adulterous relationships, father children outside of their marital covenant and continue to lead congregations. High profile Christian artists are choosing the charts over their children and wealth over their wives. Whatever happened to the idea that the family is our first and most important priority? It is a sad commentary on our modern church era; spiritual unfaithfulness and adultery seems to be the norm. Ministers are spending more time with the "wife" of another man- the church, than their own spouses and families. The church is the bride of Christ. Ministers who are more invested with Christ's bride than their own, will suffer tremendous adversity. Maybe our compulsion for prosperity and success is the culprit behind such great failure in ministerial circles. Big churches place just as much strain on a minister's marital and family life as any other endeavor; thinking that ministry work absolves them from being accountable to serving their families, or gives them license to neglect them, is a deceptive and demonic poly. Ministers must be extremely alert to the dangers of ministerial demands and the lure of success. The great stabilizer in any minister's life is a loving, caring and supportive home.

Church workers and leaders who divorce their spouses while continuing in ministry should really reevaluate their walk and work with God. Divorce and remarriage is bringing a horrible scourge on the body of Christ. There is no doubt that the church must deal with the spirit and the realities of divorce that has taken root in our culture; neither can we deny the complexity of the societal rupture on the family, but the ministry is called to a much higher standard. Some time ago, while driving, a police officer pulled me over for a routine stop. Unfortunately, I did not have all my documents on me. We talked and when I shared my occupation, she stated that both us, her as a police officer and myself as a minister, are held by higher standards than the average citizen is[14]. This is the reality for the church! There will be breakdowns and difficulties along life's often twisting and unpredictable road, and ministers are not sheltered from it, but we have a much higher standard by which we measure our actions.

What must have drove Moses was the instinctive pursuit to find himself in his familial heritage. To enter ministry and not have a foundation of his pedigree would have proved fatal in the end. He needed know where he came from and to know the God who his ancestors served. His exit from Egypt and his subsequent 40 years in the wilderness in the tents of Jethro gave him the necessary time and opportunity to find himself. He had to find himself before he could go and find God's people. His ministry is inextricably linked to his familial birthright. It was the promise to Abraham, Isaac, and Jacob that fuelled the drive to come into his own. This point may seem contradictory to the general purpose of this book, but do not be mistaken. To give ourselves away for the purpose and the cause of the Gospel demands more than just a partial commitment. If we are going to please God, we must do what is right in our own lives first. The point is that in Jewish culture, expressed in the life of both Abraham and Moses, one's family is the foundation for successful ministry. If you are a church leader, make no small plans for the things God has called you into, but be forewarned, your family is your first ministry. The saving of the souls in your own house are gifts God gives to keep you true. Those you live with know the sincerity of your walk with God. They will see your strengths, your weaknesses, your shortcomings, your failures and your successes. They see you when you are not in the pulpit, playing the music, in the office. They hear how you speak to your spouse, and treat your neighbors. The home is the place God allows His grace to forge your heart and the heart of those who live with you. Like Abraham, the commanding of your children will have far-reaching consequences. They will know to do justice and judgment because of how you model the faith.

---

[14] Yes, I did get the ticket for not having all my documents with me!

The Best Place Beyond this World: *The Heaven Team*

Jesus' earthly ministry connected uniquely to his relationship with Heaven. This connection is extremely important to our lives and our demonstration of missional spirituality. As soon as his ministry began, he drew attention to the prospects of Heaven as an intricate component to ministerial success. The inauguration of his early ministry begins with him being "…led up of the Spirit…" (Matt. 4:1). It is this "being led" that teaches us very significant lessons about working for God. God leads, we follow. Never assume God only leads beside still waters because this text reveals something quite different. He leads into wildernesses, valleys of shadows of death. While there, he is molested by the devil to abandon his heavenly team. Satan makes five attempts to lure Jesus into sin and each time Jesus thwarts the devil and secures his mission as Saviour. At the conclusion of the battle, we see ministering angels, members of the heaven team, attending to him. Be assured that faithfulness to the heaven team will guarantee us protection and security from the wiles of the devil. Let's take a few moments to explore an aspect of tremendous significance to team work in the kingdom.

Ministering Spirits

In the past several years, there has been a resurgence of belief in the supernatural world; not necessarily in the context of Christian spirituality, but we have begun to see an enormous attraction and preoccupation with angels through study and even worship. You can find books in bookstores and libraries detailing the names of angels, as well as how to draw the attention of angels into our lives. The devil has been successful in drafting a huge army of people who have bowed at this particular altar but scripture forbids the worship of angels.[15]

The study and belief in angels is no novelty in the Christian church. From the angel with the flaming sword in the Garden of Eden in the book of Genesis to the angel that showed John the New Jerusalem coming down

---

[15] www.apologeticsindex.org/2222-worship-of-angels

from heaven in the book of Revelation, the theology and belief in angels is a critical aspect of Apostolic ministry. The Bible is filled with stories of how angels aided the work of the kingdom and assisted men in their tasks.

One of my favourite accounts comes from a message I preached as a young minister. The topic of the message was *"Send Judah first"* from 2 Chronicles 20. Three rival kingdoms were attacking King Jehoshaphat. His subsequent prayer to God for help triggered a divine response. The prophet Jahaziel, brought a message from God, "You shall not need to fight in this battle, set you, stand still and see the salvation of the Lord with you…" (17). Positioned with the divine battle plan, the Jews began to praise God the next morning. The Bible reports that God set a supernatural ambush among the allied forces and they began killing each other. Although the word "angel" is not used in the text, we have strong indication that the term "the Lord" signified an "angel of the Lord". The angelic presence created confusion among the allied forces and caused them to implode. One by one, the soldiers began turning on each other until they had annihilated each other.

Another personal favourite, is the story in the book of Daniel chapter 10. Daniel's concern for his people exiled in Babylon for a determined time is compelled to go on a three week fast with prayer. At the end of the fast, Daniel has an experience that reveals to us the presence of angels aiding covenant people. Daniel reports his vision. Look what he sees! A figure clothed in linen, his waist was girded with a gold waistband, his body was hard and glistening as if sculpted from precious stone, his face was radiant, his eyes bright and penetrating like torches, his arms and feet glistening like polished bronze, and his voice deep and resonant sounding like a huge choir of voices. Daniel said this *being* touched him, raising him up from the ground after collapsing in the presence of the creature. Pulling him up, he tells Daniel he is sent to answer Daniel's prayer and fasting request. What comes next is one of the most interesting disclosures of heavenly activity in the Biblical narrative. The angel explains to Daniel that his prayers were not answered for three-weeks due to the resistance of the angel-prince over the dominion of Persia. With the aid of Michael, one of the chief angel-princes, he was liberated and able to deliver God's message to Daniel. Wow! Just when you think it is over and you have heard enough, the angel-prince says he must return and contend with another angel-prince. This time, he would confront the angel-prince over Greece.

This angelic battle reveals to us that there is assistance and interference from heavenly and human forces, each attempting to thwart the others plans. Daniel's prayer shows that humanity must depend on divine support to operate and function in service. Angels are assigned to help us in the execution of our work here on earth.

In the New Testament, the episodes are no less exciting and dramatic. In Acts 12, at the outbreak of persecution, the death of James seemed to have pleased and excited the Jewish rulers. Herod, realizing that this action had brought some popularity, sought the life of the apostle Peter. Upon his arrest and incarceration, awaiting the passing of the Passover feast, Peter is supernaturally delivered. While imprisoned and asleep under heavy guard, an angel stands by his side – awaking him, gives him instructions. "Hurry, get dressed...put on your shoes...grab your coat and let's get out of here" (verse 7-9, Message Translation). Peter thought he was in a dream. The angel led him past the guards and locked iron gates swung open without assistance. Peter is lead to the city center and there left. It is at that point that Peter realizes this is no dream; this was real. He was actually awake and an angel accompanied him to freedom. Peter is amazed at God's rescue and preservation of his life, and this becomes his victorious testimony to the saints who were praying for him all night. It is not over. The next morning, there is no small stir at the prison. No one can find Peter. Herod orders the execution of the guards, which was a common practice in the first century if prisoners escaped. It was recorded sometime after, that Herod displayed an extravagant show of arrogance and pomp. The people reveled in this pride and called him a god. The Bible records that after this display, an angel of the Lord came down from heaven and killed him. The monarch was smote with some form of disease that claimed his life. On this account, the Word of God grew and multiplied.

Here it is the heaven team, a combination of angelic and human beings working hand in hand. Time would fail us to list the powerful records of human encounters with the divine; Manoah and the angel that pronounces the birth of Samson. Jacob wrestles with the angel of the Lord; Elisha and the angels on chariots of fire; Daniel in the den of lions; angels blow trumpets and pour out bowls; Seraphims flying through the heavens shouting laudations of praise and worship; angels with swords of judgment; angels that guide; bring messages; turn nature; and so on.

Powerful ministry cannot exist without the involvement of a heavenly team.

Interacting with heaven was an important aspect of Jesus' ministry; he often retreated to connect with heaven. A deep intimacy with God and the host of ministering angels is critical for ministerial and missional success. Time spent in prayer is not only a weapon of warfare but also an important life skill that cultivates the heart of the one that prays to access the heavenly realm. I do not want to leave out the necessity of fasting, abstinence from food for a specific period in order to seek the Lord. The Bible is full of those who were able to interact with heaven on a different level because they understood the importance of fasting. I have not written to explain this important spiritual discipline but there are many great books on the subject.[16] Working on teams and with teams of people in the execution of Kingdom business will always challenge your spiritual integrity, your personal and professional will, so time with God alone is vital for renewal. The assistance of heaven is a valued element of success in ministry.

The Best Way to Serve in this World: *The Ministry Team*

In one of the most tactical moves in biblical leadership, Jesus assembles his elite team. These men are not commandos, at least not at the first. Similar to David's mighty men, they are not likely to be nominated for any of today's Fortune 500 companies or professional teams. They have not attended the best rabbinical schools, they are not graduates of the most endorsed seminaries, neither are they among the renowned sought after conference speakers. Instead, they are a band of disjointed men. Men like Levi, a publican, the disdain of Jewish society. Publicans were Jews that collected taxes for their enemies, the Romans. Some of Jesus'

---

[16] It is interesting that many people either do not believe in fasting or never been taught. I remember when I was in Bible College and met a young woman who, although she had been in church for many years had never fasted and knew very little about it. One of our lecturers was teaching on the role fasting played in the monastic periods and that it was a deep discipline of the early church. After hearing about it, she desired to learn more. I was able to spend some time instructing her and fasting with her.

team members were a part of a fundamentalist group that were seeking to overthrow the Roman government by force. Another, a skeptic; one was a brawling fisherman with an abrasive temperament and little patience. In this cohort of men, we find a secret to leadership that flies in the face of most modern day leadership theory. Jesus does not recruit the best of the best, at least not in terms of human standards. He does not look at a congregation and seek for people who come from good families, the best schools, or those who seem to have things together. He had spent all night in prayer before selecting his team. I have often wondered what it was about these men that the Holy Spirit identified with to select them for His core team. Was there something latent in them not readily seen on the surface of their personality and daily living? That prayer exercised by the Lord created the climate for him to select the twelve men that would comprise the governing ministry that would take the Gospel to the entire world, upon whose teaching the church would be erected.

Honestly, I believe we have drunk a particular doctrine of modern business language that teaches to be successful, you recruit and/or hire the best people. In our minds, those with advanced training, who hold important positions in their jobs, who can contribute financially, the most popular, talented, gifted and maybe those most connected to the right people, fall into this elite class. I must say, on one hand, looking for the best people is a fair and reasonable practice, as long as you stay within a particular operational setting; biblical principles for leadership as found in the Pastoral Epistles. However, on the other hand, we should ask ourselves, are we aspiring to do our work in the church the way Jesus did, or should we follow some other method? I have read many books on leadership, among them Maxwell's volumes, Kouze and Posner, Collins, Hybels, Sweet, and I would be ungrateful if I did not admit to the value of the lessons I have learned from these great writers and leaders. These writers have been invaluable to my own leadership understanding. However, I see something in Jesus I have not found in any of these writers and I wonder if those of us in the church are missing something. Have we replaced biblical principles and concepts with principles that are not inherently biblical, into church practice? I see in Jesus' leadership two fundamental principles that we should consider; *Maturation*, which is time to develop people and *Devotion*, which is the time needed to learn dependence on the

Holy Spirit for success. In our modern age, we deal with the time issue by simply trying to recruit and hire people that we do not have to spend a lot of time training or investing in. We want them to hit the ground running. To be honest I have fallen into that trap. This way our ministries can grow faster. Maybe there is some merit in that, but why did Jesus choose men that did not have any apparent leadership skills and were not a part of the societal elite? Why did he spend an entire night in prayer before making His selection? Now, don't get me wrong, I am not saying that they didn't have leadership skills or potential. It is obvious they had gifts in them that qualified them for this essential position. Nevertheless, they were not really functioning in that level of operation at the time of their calling. It then took three years for Jesus to direct, train, mentor and guide them to a new level of service that, once accomplished, would change the world forever.

Jesus showed us that dealing with the issue of people selection for ministry, there must be an inordinate amount of time spent in prayer. The business of the Kingdom is not possible except the King of the Kingdom enlist the people He wants in His employ. I have had my fair share of selecting people who talk a good talk, but at the first sign of trouble, they are nowhere to be found. When Jesus said, "...follow me and I will make you fishers of men..." I believe he was saying if you are going to select leaders for church ministry spend time in prayer and allow the Lord to guide your selection process. Do not just look for the "best people"; the so called, "best people" can really fool you. Somehow, the "not so best people" seem to come to the work of the Lord with a greater zeal for the work of the ministry. You see, in the Constantinian church era, the focus is on professional ministry, "best people" paradigm, popularly called clergy; your paid staff people. I am not advocating that churches do not hire people; the Bible gives ample attention to compensation of ministers and Christian workers. I am saying that we should not to believe that those hired are the keys to a growing missional apostolic church. Tapping into the potential of the unprofessional, non-clergy people was the genius behind Jesus' ministry, and should be the ruling principle behind ours. In the next section, we will give more attention to leadership issues.

There are three great examples of non-professional people called into the service of the Master. Two women whose lives were despoiled, both were caught in adulterous lifestyles and the other a wretched man. The first woman, Mary Magdalene, an adulterer, had seven devils cast out of her, (Luke 7:37) and later becomes the first person to proclaim the "resurrected Lord" (Matt. 28:1-10). How's that for unprofessional? How is that for using the base things of the earth? The other woman, a Samaritan, met Jesus at a well, through who transformation came to an entire town. Her history was fraught with infidelity and dishonor. She had four husbands and the man she was currently with, Jesus says was not her husbands. Yet, she participates in the Kingdom. Her witness is powerful. Finally, Peter, after his great exhibition of supposed faithfulness and readiness to die with the Lord, miserably fails and is driven into a regretful abyss of guilt. He is commissioned and led by the Lord to preach the first message post- Pentecost, which resulted in over 3000 souls being saved and the door being opened to the gentile world.

Jesus' entire life is characterized by choosing people who were not a part of the professional elite, society's religious upper echelon, before coming into ministry. We know many great people followed Jesus but somehow the stories captured in the Bible seem to display the lives of the unknown at the forefront of this emerging missional apostolic movement. Zacchaeus for instance, chief among the publicans or tax gatherers, superintendent of customs and tribute was among those that were extremely wealthy and influential based on societal rank, found himself in the company of the Lord, and experienced a conversion experience.[17] Then there was Joseph of Arimathea, the rich Pharisee. Prophecy had announced that Jesus would have His death among the rich. It so happened that Jesus' company was among the rich at His death (Isa 53:9). Joseph, one of those silent disciples that because of fear did not publicly acknowledge faith in the Master, but he possessed the wherewithal to purchase a new tomb on a parcel of land in which to place the body of Jesus. We don't uncover these characters at first glance; instead they are buried deep in the text, as if to hide their value. The lessons are clear though: Jesus used people in frontline ministry that possessed the character traits of the simple. In the church where I serve as pastor, my team has attempted to encroach upon the Pareto principle. The Pareto principle "...states that, for many events, roughly 80% of the effects come from 20% of the causes"[18] or 20% of the people do 80% of

---

[17] (Fausset's Bible Dictionary, Electronic Database Copyright (c)1998 by Biblesoft n.d.)

[18] http://en.wikipedia.org/wiki/Pareto_principle

the work. It seems like the clergy-laity matrix falls right smack in the center of this theory. I think we should challenge that theory. Can you imagine a church that inverts this principle and has 80% of people, each doing 20% of the work? If everyone did a little, revival would break out, many doing little versus a few doing a lot. Maybe I am being over ambitious, even impractical, to suggest that we could violate a proven law, but why not. Peter walked on water. Really, think about it. If every member in the body, your church, moved in some way to touch a human life for Christ, can you imagine the outcome?

What we really need to do is re-examine our assumptions about the people of God and begin to enlist, train, and develop *all* the people for the work of the ministry. J. Paul Getty once said "it is better to have 1% of 100 people than to have 100% of 1 person" referring to himself. The concept is applicable to the church as well. It is better to have a little from everyone working for the Lord, than to have a lot from one or a few. We must stop thinking that ordained officers, and highly skilled people are the answer to the churches expansion and growth problems. No intelligent person will rule out the importance of leadership in the development of a missional apostolic church. The issue is how we build a culture of leadership around *all* the people of God. For centuries, the concept of the priesthood of all believers has only been a theological proposition. The professional clergy rules in the operation of the church. A truly authentic apostolic church must release *all* the people to do the work of the ministry. Many churches modeled on a Christendom system (a church system that developed during the post-apostolic era) must break from that system and challenge people to contribute to the expansion of the church. We see how Jesus did this. Jesus called people to a very deep commitment. Commitment, I think is very scarce in most churches today. Among established churches, the ones that have galvanized their congregations to grow are usually churches that require a great commitment from *all* its members to be in some way responsible for reaching lost people. It may be a good idea, if church leaders desire to reach more people for Christ, that they challenge themselves, their churches, and the leaders, to all commit to the task; they should create a culture that keeps at its heart the responsibility for growth on all people, not just the church leadership. Can you imagine what would happen?

CHAPTER 2

The Indispensable Quality of Following Jesus: Commitment

One of the serious maladies in many contemporary churches in the West is the lack of committed saints. We have become committed to church buildings, the pastor[19] or the church's reputation. As a pastor, I have noticed that people who visit our church tend to be more interested in what our vision statement is than what the church believes and what the church's mission is. I believe you have to have a vision because it is a picture of the future; however, vision without mission is just a wish, an empty dream. I

---

[19] I don't want to sound like I am dishonouring the office of the pastor, I am one. It is a bit concerning to me how the "pastor" has become so intricate to the life of the church over and above any other office or gift. The personality of the pastor has almost more weight than the person of Christ. However, my study of the New Testament has caused me to grow cautious of the influence that has developed around this office over the years; especially in exclusion to the other five fold ministries. In fact, I don't think there is a denomination that is excluded from this distortion. Unless a pastor carries an anointing and gifting for outreach, most times they are unable to grow and expand the kingdom by themselves. It is essential that the church have those with other gifting to contribute to the expansion of the church, the organization or denomination. The office or gift of the pastor is not given to handle the kind of expansion God requires. His/her role is to shepherd the flock. To feed the saints through teaching, creating a spiritually healthy environment, and helping them to develop spiritual disciplines. For the most part pastors are not necessarily given to expand the church. Paul was an expander, a missionary; therefore, his pastoral duties where limited and even caused challenges to his authority among some of the churches, (see 2 Corinthians and Paul's defense of his apostleship).

have come to understand that vision keeps you going after you have served hard in the day-to-day rudiments of life, which is the mission itself.

Jesus' building process was so deeply entrenched in excellence and self-sacrifice that he called for an extremely high level of commitment from every disciple. Following Jesus was not a walk in the park. It would take men from their families, women from their homes and for some, it meant radical career changes. Levi, also known as Matthew, walked away from a lucrative enterprise to follow Jesus. James and John left their father's business without notice in order to follow the Messiah. Jesus was serious about who was going to follow him. Nowhere, do we see Jesus complying with easy commitment levels. He doesn't send the disciples back to plan an exit strategy for leaving their father's business. He doesn't tell Matthew to ensure he has a package before leaving the receipt of customs. Even more striking, He makes no promise upfront of any benefits to the task. In one place, He tells them that they will be betrayed by family members, persecuted by fellow countrymen and threatened by foreigners. Let's shed this beautiful, placid picture that we have of Jesus that doesn't challenge us at the deepest, most heartfelt places. A picture of Jesus working with us to build consensus or compromise is one of the most dangerous schemes of the enemy; this may work well in the political arena but not in the Kingdom of God. In the Kingdom, Jesus is the Ruler, King, Judge and Warrior of righteousness. He is a sovereign, and his word is absolute and final. Whatever picture you have of Jesus will more than likely shape the attitude in which you approach his service. Probably the best way for us to understand him is to ensure that we see him in all of his forms and ministries. In one scene, he is a stern parent or leader, disciplining his children. In another, He is the picture of an expectant father awaiting the return of a lost son, yet, another time, He is a loving father embracing some playful children on his lap.

It is not so much the actual picture that we have in mind, as what those images portray, that bears the most meaning. How many of us have the images of Jesus as a warrior, covered in blood from doing battle with the enemy? This is the image one prophet sees when he declares…

> *"Who is this that cometh from Edom, with dyed garments*
> *from Bozrah? this that is glorious in his apparel, travelling*
> *in the greatness of his strength? I that speak in righteousness,*

mighty to save. **Wherefore art thou red in thine apparel, and thy garments like him that treadeth in the winefat? I have trodden the winepress alone; and of the people there was none with me: for I will tread them in mine anger, and trample them in my fury; and their blood shall be sprinkled upon my garments, and I will stain all my raiment.** *For the day of vengeance is in mine heart, and the year of my redeemed is come. And I looked, and there was none to help; and I wondered that there was none to uphold: therefore mine own arm brought salvation unto me; and my fury, it upheld me". Isa 63:1-6*

The garments are dyed with blood, and not His own blood. The blood is from the war with the armies of the enemies of the Messiah who have chased the Jewish people from Jerusalem to Bozrah. Do you see this image of Jesus? Or, do you see a weak lamb, beaten, broken, and silent in the face of his enemy? I contend that you need to see both the lamb led to the slaughter and the warrior coming out of Bozrah, but they don't exist at the same time.

If you are going to follow Jesus, you are going to put everything on the line. Make no mistake about it. To follow him, you must become like a lamb while understanding what it will take to become a warrior. This is depicted in Clint Eastwood's *Grand Torino*. Eastwood plays the character Mr. Walt, an old war hero who sacrifices himself for his young friend, and his family. This was a classic example of the power of sacrifice. One thing all the epic stories teach us is that warriors are intimately connected to their king, be it an idea, a set of principles or a monarch.

The writer John Eldridge sums it up as the other side of the warrior soul, the Christian who is serious about his walk with God, his need to *know* his King and how that relationship drives him, when he writes,

"If you're not pursuing a dangerous quest with your life, well, then you don't need a Guide. If you haven't found yourself in the midst of a ferocious war, then you won't need a seasoned Captain. If you've settled in your mind to live as though this is a fairly neutral world and you are simply trying to live your life as best you can, then you can probably get by with the Christianity

of tips and techniques....But if you intend to live in the Story that God is telling, and if you want the life he offers, then you are going to need more than a handful of principles, however noble they may be. There are too many twists and turns in the road ahead, too many ambushes waiting only God knows where, too much at stake. You cannot possibly prepare yourself for every situation. Narrow is the way, said Jesus. How shall we be sure to find it? We need God intimately, and we need him desperately."[20]

Let's take a closer look at Jesus' call to commitment and don't think for a minute this does not apply to you. If you feel challenged or even frightened as you read these cases, I have made my point. Ask God for a fresh baptism of fire and adventure because the church[21] has all but killed this level of commitment in its disciples. If we endeavour to occupy ourselves with the task of recovering the revolutionary character of Jesus at this level, we will recover the mission. If we recover the mission, we will encounter Jesus the revelator[22]. Let's take a look at 7 indispensable cases of commitment.

---

[20] Eldridge, John. The Heart: *Waking the Dead*, Thomas Nelson Press, 2007. Nashville Tennessee

[21] When I use the term church here I am dealing with how The Church has fallen so far from her calling, not living its true apostolic identity, adapting a foreign attitude towards kingdom building; she has taken away the seriousness of commitment in challenging the saints to give their all to God and His service.

[22] Revolution, revelation and recovery are essential concepts in following Jesus of Nazareth. The church has lost the sense of revolution; fearful of being controversial we have accepted the tranquillizing drug of toleration. The state religious system of Christendom has affected the apostolic churches to its core. We must recapture the revolutionary ministry of Jesus. Revelation remains key to our ministry practice. Many in the church have attempted to use rationalization to understand the deep things of God. Yes, we must be thinkers, but we must depend deeply on the work of the Holy Spirit to reveal his mind to us, especially in pioneering new ministry, where revelation is needed. It is not so much revelation for doctrinal clarity we seek but for ministry implementation. The apostolic church must recover the practices of the early church. Although much less sophisticated they were embedded with the gene of power from Jesus, less need for technology because the spirit didn't need that for its work. We must recover the heart of Jesus, the passion of Christ, the Zeal of the Lord.

SEVEN CALLS TO COMMITMENT

1. Follow me

And he saith unto them, Follow me[23], and I will make you fishers of men (Mt. 4:19).

When Jesus called his disciples, it was a call into a mentorship relationship, a lifestyle of ministry. One of the disciples, asked the Lord who would be the greatest among them. Jesus' response was not to discourage the pursuit of greatness, but instead to put ambition and greatness into perspective. For too long, many in the Christian church have shied away from any leaning to true greatness, but Jesus simply responds by saying the one who will be great is the one who will serve. In other words, you can become great, you can stand out from a crowd, and yes, you can lead, but you must become a servant. You will give yourself to the cause of Christ by serving others with your gifts; you must give yourself away, only then will you be great. You want to be great? No problem! Serve!

The disciples would spend three years walking with him across the countryside, seeing miracles; the dead raised, crippled people healed, and demons cast out of people. One great depiction of someone being called is seen in the life of Matthew. His is one who immediately responded when Jesus called him to follow. He seeks no advice or counsel from friend or family; he wastes no time in considering his career but rather immediately walks away from a lucrative job to follow this rabbi called Jesus. Now, what did you and I do when God called us? Did we drop everything and follow or did we have some long bout of resistance, intellectual reasoning, and social ponderings to satiate our consciousness? Did you have to seek approval from a spouse, a parent, a friend, a co-worker? It has been said and proven that those who can make decisions quickly will meet with greater success than those who must ponder a decision for a long time. People usually resort to their failure comfort zone with the following words, "I'll think about it". Here is a quote retelling the infamous interview between

---

[23] Matthew 9:9; 19:21; Mk 2:14; Lk. 5:27; 9:59: Jn. 1:43; 21:22

Andrew Carnegie and Napoleon Hill as told by Keith Matthew of self-mastery secrets[24].

Andrew Carnegie had offered Napoleon Hill the opportunity to interview America's wealthiest people to create a success system. He secretly held a stopwatch in his pocket and gave young Napoleon no more than 60 seconds to decide. Napoleon Hill came back with a resounding "yes" 32 seconds later and the rest is history. Having listened to Napoleon Hill's recorded talks countless times, I knew the importance of being decisive.

It seems to me that the people in the Bible, who often made great impact, were decisive when called by God. They responded quickly and began working for the Lord. Consider the following applications: Paul on the road to Damascus, Isaiah and his King Uzziah experience, Matthew and his call from the tax table, David and the encounter with Goliath, Abraham taking Isaac to worship, Abigail and her action to thwart David's anger, Rahab and the spies, and these are but a few. None of these examples deny that there was tension, but something must be said for that inner ability to be decisive.

This point couldn't be made any clearer in terms of the call of the apostles. In Matthew 4:19-22, we see the call and response of Peter, Andrew, James and John to Jesus. Matthew records that Peter and Andrew followed straightway.

> *"And he saith unto them, Follow me, and I will make you fishers of men: And they **straightway left their nets**, and followed him."*

Then he records the experiences of James and John as an act of immediacy.

> *"And going on from thence, he saw other two brethren, James the son of Zebedee, and John his brother, in a ship with Zebedee their father, mending their nets; and **he called them: And they immediately left the ship and their father**, and followed him."*

---

[24] http://www.selfmasterysecrets.com/success/what-napoleon-hill-and-andrew-carnegie-taught-me-about-opportunity/

How different is this from many in the church today. Some of us would say, "Hey Jesus! Let me stay with my dad and make some money and then I can support the ministry with all the money that I make". Somehow, unlike modern times, these men saw and esteemed walking with Jesus as greater riches than what they could have attained on the fishing boat. It is in that single decision to walk with Jesus that they enrolled in the School of "turning the world upside down" Institute.

I don't want to give the impression that there is nothing to gain in following the Lord. Jesus told his disciple that the reward for forsaking everything was to receive great gain. In Matthew 19, Matthew records Jesus' comforting his disciples regarding their reward. This reward is not only for the twelve but for all those who will follow the Lord.

> *"Then answered Peter and said unto him, Behold, we have forsaken all, and followed thee; what shall we have therefore? And Jesus said unto them, Verily I say unto you, That ye which have followed me, in the regeneration when the Son of man shall sit in the throne of his glory, ye also shall sit upon twelve thrones, judging the twelve tribes of Israel. **And every one that hath forsaken houses, or brethren, or sisters, or father, or mother, or wife, or children, or lands, for my name's sake, shall receive an hundredfold, and shall inherit everlasting life.**"*

This is an awesome promise. For too long, the Christian church has developed a deposition to poverty and making poverty a virtue. If you analyze the question, you would see Peter's genuine desire to know what the reward for service was. We would naturally expect some super spiritual answer. However, Jesus' word was that they, and all believers beyond the era of the disciples, would be rewarded a hundredfold and would receive everlasting life. Somewhere along the line, many in the church have forsaken the hope and expectation of everlasting life and have devoted themselves one hundred percent to a totally materialist worldview. I think that we need to give ourselves to a more honest view of last things. If the earth is the Lord's and the fullness thereof, and at the end of time there will be a new Jerusalem coming down from heaven, somewhere in our theology there has to be an understanding that the earth, and all its resources, treasures, beauty and splendor, is a part of our reward. What we have to guard ourselves from is the world's system, a system that has at its source, material elements that gives us meaning and value. The problem is that all material things will decay and fade away. A worldly system has no place in our preoccupation, but Jesus' words tell us to have a more endearing desire.

2. Not everyone is fit...

> *"And he said unto another, Follow me. But he said, Lord, suffer me first to go and bury my father. Jesus said unto him,* **Let the dead bury their dead**: *but go thou and preach the kingdom of God. And another also said, Lord, I will follow thee; but let me first go bid them farewell, which are at home at my house. And Jesus said unto him,* **No man, having put his hand to the plough, and looking back, is fit for the kingdom of God**. *Luke 9:59-62"*

Our wealth of earthly wisdom wants to reject these sentiments of the Lord, but if we are really going to follow the Lord we must understand his teaching and concede. Somehow, the greater call for progressive experiences and achievements are not possible without people making decisions backed up with demonstrated action, which is a barometer of our faith. These actions sometimes will require the highest level of sacrifice and, at times, may even seem insensitive and uncaring. At other times, they may seem downright disrespectful, but this is the demand of the call of God on people's lives. It was H.W. Longfellow who said, "Heights of great men reached and kept, were not attained by sudden flight but they while their companions slept, were toiling upwards in the night" [25] There is no great achievement of any worthy recognition if people have not made sacrifices in the assent of the most noblest of endeavours. Frankly, there is no greater endeavour than the work of the Gospel. Although people are called to many activities where they spend their time and gain a living, there is nothing more worthy of a person's effort than obedience to the call of God upon their life.

---

[25] http://www.brainyquote.com/quotes/quotes/h/henrywadsw129800.html

Many ministers want great churches with little or no effort. Many saints want the power of God without much prayer and many people want recognition without service. There are things that must be done in order to be fit for the Kingdom of God. Again, I challenge you to know the will of God for your life. Make a quality decision and then begin to work with passion, drive, determination, persistence and vision without looking back. The church must be such a place where seeds of enormous potentiality are cultivated. The people in our churches are vessels with majestic treasure in them. The days in which we live don't call for the gentle pouring of ourselves out for the nations, but a breaking, so that the precious essential oil of the Spirit can flow from us and change the lives of men and women[26].

Jesus could not really mean what he was saying! I think most are quick to dismiss the "let the dead bury the dead" statement. We justify that he could not really mean that. Some causes in life call people to tremendous sacrifices. Men have volunteered to go war, with young children and wife at home, knowing there were no guarantees of return. These are men that risk their lives for something greater than themselves. Jesus is saying if you cannot see the work of the kingdom greater than anything here on earth, you *are not fit* for the kingdom.

3. Drink blood and eat flesh

> *"I am that bread of life: Your fathers did eat manna in the wilderness, and are dead. This is the bread which cometh down from heaven, that a man may eat thereof, and not die.* **I am the living bread which came down from heaven: if any man eat of this bread, he shall live forever: and the bread that I will give is my flesh, which I will give for the life of the world.** *The Jews therefore strove among themselves, saying, How can this man give us his flesh to eat? Then Jesus said unto them, Verily, verily, I say unto you,* **Except ye eat the flesh of the Son of man, and drink his blood, ye have no life in you. Whoso eateth my flesh, and drinketh my**

---

[26] Mark 14:1-3

blood, hath eternal life; and I will raise him up at the last day. For my flesh is meat indeed, and my blood is drink indeed. He that eateth my flesh, and drinketh my blood, dwelleth in me, and I in him. As the living Father hath sent me, and I live by the Father: so he that eateth me, even he shall live by me. This is that bread which came down from heaven: not as your fathers did eat manna, and are dead: he that eateth of this bread shall live forever. These things said he in the synagogue, as he taught in Capernaum. Many therefore of his disciples, when they had heard this, said, this is a hard saying; who can hear it? When Jesus knew in himself that his disciples murmured at it, he said unto them, Doth this offend you? What and if ye shall see the Son of man ascend up where he was before? It is the spirit that quickeneth; the flesh profiteth nothing: the words that I speak unto you, they are spirit, and they are life" (John 6:48-69)

It is difficult to find many leaders intentionally doing things that will drive people away from their ministries. These days it seems like ministers are more concerned about not offending people in hopes that they will stay in their churches. Bishop S.A Dunn, the great Apostolic preacher to the United Kingdom, once said that the churches that allow the offering plate to determine what happens in the church will ceased being faithful to the calling of God. He was right in that declarative and prophetic statement. The popularizing of the Gospel without offending people may cause growth, but such growth doesn't ignite sacrificial commitment of its adherents. Jesus challenges his followers with such extravagant confrontations that he reduces his membership greatly. Consider this story. Jesus begins to teach about the value of life and how the life he spoke of would be transmitted. Among other things, this is a lesson on commitment. He turns to the crowd and says to them, *"Except ye eat the flesh of the Son of man, and drink his blood, ye have no life in you. Whoso eateth my flesh, and drinketh my blood, hath eternal life";* silence sweeps over the group and conflicting thoughts rush through the minds of these hopeful disciples. Once the word has had the chance to settle, the crowd of disciples begins to dwindle away. One by one, they turn their back on the man that they hoped would be the answer to Israel's hopes. There is no record that Jesus attempts to reclaim these men to his ministry. He simply turns to the 12 remaining disciples and asks if they planned to leave as well. Peter's response demonstrates to us insight into what is required of those who will follow the Master and do the kind of things that will reach a dying world. He says "Lord, to whom shall we go? Thou hast the words of eternal life. And **we believe and are sure** that thou art that Christ, the Son of the living God "(John 6:68-69).

Jesus' strategy is intentional; it shifts those whose motives for following him were less than pure. Jesus knew that where he was leading them, they were going to have to make sacrifices at the highest levels. There would be no easy walk with Jesus. He wanted to know if they had what it took to weather the storms of Apostolic ministry, what Paul calls "...the afflictions of the Gospel..." (2 Tim.1:8). He wasn't speaking to their current state of maturity as leaders and disciples. He was testing their long-term resolve, their capacity for complexity, and their ability to stick during hard times. Sometimes it's better to have the wrong people "off the bus"[27] early so you don't waste time with them in the long run. Some people are good at causing you to waste time with mundane issues, problems and questions. Sometimes their presence is a sign that you are not far enough in your journey and, to step into that next level, they must go. Therefore, Peter's statement, "we believe and are sure..." suggests that he was ready for a paradigm shift. What a lofty statement Peter makes; no one understood what Jesus had just taught. However strange, there was something in Peter and the other eleven that would not let them depart from following Jesus.

---

[27] Jim Collins book "Good To Great and the Social Sectors: A monograph to Accompany Good to Great; Why Business Thinking is not the answer, masterfully applied the finding from his business research to the social sector and recognized that the right people were critical for sustaining long term growth. His phrase "off the bus" referred to the discipline of having the right people on the team and the wrong people off. Jesus' method of determining the right people was based in selecting people who were willing to demonstrate commitment, not based on egoism or economics but sheer desire for virtue, those who sought a nobility of service and meaning. In the social sector however, it is more difficult to remove the wrong people based on the organizational socio-relational elements or tenured positions. I have found when you remove people from positions in the church they don't leave the church and if they are unhappy about the decision to replace them it creates problems ongoing with relationships in the church.

You have to be convinced that Jesus is the Christ if you are going to follow him. Now, you may not recognize this, but this is a serious challenge to your faith. Things that Jesus will say will rub you completely the wrong way. If you are not ready, you too may walk away.

Interesting enough, these words still carry the same weight that they did nearly 2000 years ago. The only difference is that it is a bit easier to hide behind a false sense of commitment today than in the first century. Seventeen centuries of Christianity has lulled us into a very apathetic understanding of Christian commitment.. Tolerance has really done us in. George Barna, a Christian research specialist, reported that the idea of a faith of integrity and honest devotion has been completely shattered. Christians who surveyed and whom identified themselves with orthodoxy reported some revealing data that should allow us to see how far we are from a truly impassioned church.

His report found that:

- Half of "born-again Christians" believe that the Ten Commandments are irrelevant.
- Nearly half concur that the idea of sin is outdated concluding that only 17 percent of all born-again Christians surveyed retained a biblical view on all survey statements.
- More recently, these research findings in a 2002 poll on the same subject found that the divorce rate is no different for born-again Christians than for those who do not consider themselves religious.
- Interestingly, most Christian votes are influenced more by economic self-interest than by spiritual and moral values. (We never had to say this before, but now we have to add ethnic identification; I am sure that the election of the 43rd President of the United States saw born again Christians that were more excited about the significance of his skin colour then his values.)
- Finally, the desire of having a close, personal relationship with God ranks sixth among the twenty-one life goals tested among the born again, trailing such desires as "living a comfortable lifestyle"[28].

---

[28] Csorba, Les. *Trust: the one thing that makes or breaks a leader.* Thomas Nelson Press, 2004. Chapter 8: "The Affair" pages 134-145.

"I am a Christian", bears less and less meaning in the world we live in today – everyone is a Christian. Are you in a position to partake in the suffering and dying of the Lord Jesus Christ? Are you willing to "eat his flesh" and "drink his blood"? If not, you have not gone far enough yet. You have not been challenged enough yet! Christianity is more than a label we wear as a symbol of our religious affiliation; it is a calling into the suffering of Jesus Christ

4. Fox holes, birds nests and no place to sleep

"And a certain scribe came, and said unto him, Master, I will follow thee whithersoever thou goest. And Jesus saith unto him, The foxes have holes, and the birds of the air have nests; but the Son of man hath not where to lay his head" Matthew 8:19-20; Luke 9:58

Any minister that has been in the ministry for any length of time has had the experience of people coming into his office and promising that they are 100% with the ministry and that they are 100% in support of the leader. Ironically when challenges surface these individuals are nowhere to be found. Often people over commit themselves to the call of the ministry. They're either trying to impress someone, usually the pastor, or they are trying to convince themselves that they are a fearless committed believer. I have learned it is less important to listen to what people say than to watch what they do. Somehow, actions speak volumes as to a person's motives, values and heart. A leader that watches and discerns, needs time to adequately observe people and judge the fruits of their behavior.

One day, an unnamed disciples comes to Jesus with a sense of pride that he is willing to go anywhere with the Lord. The omniscience of the Lord searches into the soul of this ill-equipped disciple and, with the love and concern for him to one day be all that he desires, Jesus' response to him is that "foxes have holes and birds of the air have nests but the son of Man have not where to lay his head". In these words, the Lord is asking

"Do you have the capacity to attend with me even though I don't have anywhere to lay my head at nights? I have nothing to give you, nothing to pay you. We will move from place to

place and not be there long enough to establish any lasting associates. In some places we will be despised, in others we will be ignored, and worse, in some places the threat to our very lives will be great. You will go without food, shelter, friendship and love. In some instances we will have to escape for our lives and at other times we will feel lonely and without peace. We will make attempts to do the work of God and be unsuccessful, we will be laughed at, ridiculed, and some of us will even lose our lives".

I like being around people who are not afraid to be challenged, people who are indifferent to creature comforts and can be cool in any situation. Emergent leaders desire fellowship with men and women who are not afraid to dream impossible dreams. Without sounding sadistic, Jesus seems to say if we are going to experience a true Apostolic movement we must be willing to recognize that there will be sacrifices made that do not accompany the comforts that foxes have in their holes or the comforts that birds have in their nests. I am not advocating intentionally not taking care of home life or acquiring possessions. The call at this level must cause one to consider the risks and dangers of going on the field and doing ministry, the necessity to be sold out, a deep-seated divine discontentment, where your spirit is so full of the desire for a move of God, that it disrupts the normal course of everyday life.

5. Go into all the world

Go ye therefore, and teach all nations, baptizing them in the name of the Father, and of the Son, and of the Holy Ghost: Teaching them to observe all things whatsoever I have commanded you: and, lo, I am with you always, even unto the end of the world. Amen. (Matt 28:19-20)

One group that has positioned themselves for expansive ministry and developed a strong missional culture is the United Pentecostal Church International. They have been affective in creating a great commission focus and have embedded this into the entire fabric of organizational operations. For many Apostolics, this has left many disillusioned with their own sense of ministerial purpose and understanding. All of us are called to obedience to the commission, if there are groups that have accomplished the mandate of Jesus Christ, we can and should take their example as an indication of what is possible. When I was growing up, I was an avid athlete, I played every sport. When I came to a sport I had never played before, all I needed to see was someone else play. Once that happened, I knew I could play too, or at least give it a shot. That is how we should be in ministry. The UPCI have and are leading the way in many respects in accomplishing the Great Commission. There is no need for us to stand back and watch. If they can do it, so can others. In my personal experience as a new catalytic church planter,[29] I have been bombarded with statements to the effect that, someone else is doing it, so why bother. The statements I have found myself having to justify for new church plants are, "aren't other Pentecostal groups there?" or "are you sure that other Pentecostal groups don't have churches there?", and other statements to that effect. These are perhaps salutary statements when looked at through the prism of other organizations, which have identified themselves as church planting, evangelistic, and missional organizations. On the other hand, it seems to abdicate our responsibility in the business of church planting regardless of who else is doing it. Albert Einstein was quoted as saying, "Great spirits have always found violent opposition from mediocre minds". Are we not all to be church planting, evangelistic, and missional in our practice of the church? It is obvious that these attitudes come from individuals and churches that are void of a missional understanding as its core objective.

Why don't most churches give birth to daughter churches and support grand-daughter works? The answer may seem harsh: most churches are barren! How can the bride of Christ not produce children? I believe every

---

[29] Catalytic Church Planter – a term I coined to explain a pastor engaged in initiating new churches through and by recruiting and placement of actual church planters. Churches and leaders who envision their ministry in the capacity of birthing new churches and sending church planters to lead them are catalytic. They will not spend long terms on the field but will support the work from a distance. Traditionally, this role is attributed to Bishops, but in the emerging Great Commission church the need to possess this title is not that important.

church within a life cycle of its existence should give birth to another church. Any divergence to this is proof of a barren womb with no faith to produce seed. It is sad to say that many churches don't produce because they were conceived without a womb, and may not have been truly born of God. For a church to exist and never give birth to another work in an entire generation, seems incongruous with the natural flow of life. If the church is a living organism, she is built to reproduce. Forget the notion that a church has to be big to reproduce. Quite interestingly, some of the largest babies come from very small women. A church doesn't have to be large to give birth. The church has to have a vision that is kingdom oriented. Let me share some points that may encourage churches and leaders to recover some virility and desire children. It would be a wonderful thing to repeat the experience of Abraham and Sarah in churches in this era; to birth children out of a dead womb, made alive by the promise and power of God.

Barren Wombs

In an excellent book, *Church Planting*[30] Dr. Dag Heward-Mills talks about the dynamics of churches that are barren. He shares the five Hebrew words that translate "barren" or "barrenness" and we get a clear view of our modern church predicament by looking at these words. They are *Aqar, Shakol, Melechah, Otser* and *Tsiyah*. Let's look at them individually.

Non-Reproducing Churches

Aqar (Ex.23:26) means 'the destruction or removal of generative organs' and may even mean to have 'non-functioning organs'. Churches or denominations affected by *Aqar* are bodies that are deficient in reproducing new churches. These bodies may have many programs and activities, lots of internal social intimacy among members, but a sterile womb and the abilities to bear fruit in effective outreach, locally or internationally is absent. The deception here is that individuals in the church may be very active; participating in many church programs but the involvement and

---

[30] Heward-Mills, Dag. *Church Planting*, Parchment House, Accra Ghana, 2004

obedience to the Great Commission is deficient. The reproductive organ or the church is *Aqar*. All of the churches resources go into maintaining community within that assembly. Not a bad thing at all, however, this limits their ability to cast a vision for missiological effectiveness.

Miscarrying Church

Next is **Shakol** (Lev. 26:22) meaning "to miscarry, to suffer abortion, to be bereaved of children, to be barren, to cast your young, to make childless and to be deprived of children". This barrenness is twofold. On one hand, this body cannot retain the children born to her. As people are saved in the church, or if they give birth to other churches, they are miscarried. The ability to retain the people given is deficient.

Let's look a little closer to *Shakol* in the natural. One interesting fact of research[31] is that around 60-70% of all pregnancies, recognized and unrecognized, are lost. Research results show that because the pregnancies are lost so early, usually within the first 12 weeks, many of the women may not even have known they were pregnant. I think it is important to note that things that happen in the natural world often shadow what happens in the spirit world. So think about this: 60 -70% of potential church plants and programs for the expansion of the kingdom are lost, and the women, the churches, are unaware of it. It is one thing to abort your seed intentionally, it is another thing entirely, not to even know you have been pregnant and lose it. How does this happen? The first thing is that the church engages in the life giving process of worship every gathering. Gifts, talents, ministries, ideas and anointing are planted in the hearts of believers during times of heartfelt worship and release. However, if the church is not responsible or thoughtful, it takes no consideration of the life conceived in it. For example, when a husband and wife engage in the life giving process there is always the knowledge of the possibility that conception can take place. Usually, the woman only recognizes something is amiss if she begins to get sick or misses her menstrual cycle. However, in the cases where a heartbeat is detected, the chances of miscarriage are 5% less likely. How

---

[31] Source: www.medicinet.com/miscarriage/article.html

many churches have been lost? How many missional programs have gone unnoticed, buried in the heart of an ignored believer who drifted away or sits silently in the pews each Sunday and other worship events, watching those who are active in the house ministry? However, if the heart of a missional desire is detected, the possibilities of a ministry birth much greater. Oh, that we would detect life much sooner in our churches!

What causes miscarriages? Research reports that there are several causes for miscarriages. Among them are chromosomal abnormalities, collagen vascular disease, such as lupus, diabetes, other hormonal problems, infection and congenital abnormalities of the uterus. However, the most common cause is chromosomal abnormalities. I believe there is a link here to our problems in the church. Chromosomes are microscopic components of every cell in the body that carry all of the genetic materials that determines all physical characteristics of the person such as hair colour, eye colour, size, and skin complexion. Our overall make-up and appearance is derived from our DNA. When there is a problem in the DNA development, miscarriages can take place. What is growing inside does not match what the host is, so the body rejects it. Liken this to church groups that care little for the great commission and gifts that are birthed. The churches' DNA is incompatible with the great commission and therefore purges itself of the potential ministry offspring. What has been conceived[32] in a dynamic worship environment is a zeal for mission, a desire for expansion, a hunger for revival, but the host is stagnant, dead, debilitated and cannot contain the life in it, therefore it miscarries. Research also confirms that chromosomal abnormalities and miscarriages are far more likely in older women, 35 years old and older, than in younger women. We will discuss this again later in the book, but it is significant enough to address partially now. The older a movement or church, the more likely it is for miscarriages to take place. The body politic are sluggish, decisions take much longer to make, and power struggles may exist among influencers

---

[32] It is impossible to think about this only in the light of missiology. It is the birth of gifts that are miscarried. They are vast and diverse. Prayer ministries are also miscarried; healing ministries, faith ministries and the list could go on. All are for the enhancement of the kingdom of God. God's seed is planted, and in every seed lies the potential for which God intended. However, he sows those seeds into the church, his bride. She must carry the seed and deliver the child.

who may have ulterior motives in the ministry, and fighting for leadership positions, even when they are long past the ability to lead. I have seen some hurtful miscarriages take place. In many cases, an organization is focused on its victories of yester year, the nostalgia of the past, that most of the ministry' time is spent trying to relive the "good old days". The ministry fails to see that it is better to give birth than to maintain or resurrect life, at least where church systems are concerned. Another fact of research is that miscarriages in the second trimesters are far more serious than first trimester miscarriages. The fetus is more developed and the rupture to the body is more stressful. A church that is more than 30 years old, can be seen as living in the second trimester; if it stopped or never had a missional drive in its DNA, any new person full of zeal and fervor for the things of God will likely be challenged with tremendous organizational blockage.

Think about this: when did many organizations, denominations, or churches have their greatest growth? Was it not in the early years when the ministry was emerging? The zeal, the fire and the energy was high. Ideas flowed, the Spirit was rich with innovation, risks of enormous proportions were taken, ministers stood up against great opposition, and in the end, they prevailed. Organizations were birthed, churches were planted, young couples, who are now the seasoned men and women, were sent out, houses were sold, and small children grew up only knowing church life and sacrifice. Then the church becomes old, stale, hard, insensitive to innovation, fearful of risk, crushed by opposing views, remanded into silence and becomes a fragment of what once was. What happened here?

Decades ago during the baby boom period, families had 10, 12, 16 children. Now, however, families have one, maybe two, child(ren) and maybe a dog. This is almost analogous to the situation in the church today verses years ago. In the early part of the century, churches birthed like wildfire, revivals swept the land, but now, churches are content with one of two extremes. Either they seek the status of the mega churches, traversing dangerously close to a prostitution of the gospel and ministry to build bigger and bigger churches/ministries or they disdain the ministry philosophy of the big church, of mega ministries and use this to justify their lack of growth. These churches eventually produce or reproduce very little by way of church planting and growth. Keep in mind that this conversation has little to do with big buildings; we are talking about a missional spirit.

The other side of this barrenness is bodies that kill their young. When a young maverick or nonconformist tries to spread his or her wings, they are clipped because they are often seen as a threat to the established body. The leadership is unable to discern the Spirit, refusing to assist this person in a discipleship capacity that can help the church grow. Actually, they usually embody a spirit that was prevalent in the early days of the church, if training and support is given, these young leaders would be keys to long-term continuity of the Gospel and missions.

A Living but Dead Church

Next is **Melechah** (2 Kings 2:19-22) meaning 'a salted land, a desert or a barren land'. Here the land is dead, having no ability to produce fruit. Seeds of any kind that go into it dies. You will notice that churches and organizations continue to have yearly general assemblies, convocations, conferences, they bring in great and notable speakers who release the anointed word of God into these churches, and year after year these church bodies see little to no growth; perhaps because they are 'salted lands'. Too often the belief is that big meetings create sustainability. Often these meetings do the exact opposite, especially if they have little to no strategy behind them. Many older leaders seem unable to discern that times and people have changed. Their inability to interact with people on a new level of thinking causes a great amount of disharmony. Generational gaps increase in worldviews and prospective, and these churches experience little to no significant change, leaving two generations discontented and frustrated. In 2 Kings 2:19-22, the prophet Elisha pronounced a healing over the land. In the same manner God must heal the land of a barren church in this condition.

The Hold Back Church

Next is **Otser** (Prov. 30:16) meaning "to enclose, to hold back and to maintain, to close up, to restrain, and retain". It can also mean, "to shut up, to withhold and to stop". This is a very interesting kind of barrenness. You will find it in two forms in a church; first, in the people of that church, and secondly, with a church body. The first scenario, people in the church are gifted, even anointed, but refuse to release their gifts into the church and ministry. They will find time for everything in the community and give themselves to great and noble things but will not give themselves to the church for advancement. Sadly, they will see and know that the church is in need of their skill, talent and gifting but refuse to give themselves. I have seen churches suffer as these people refuse to give themselves to the work, and watch as the church struggles. In my own ministry tenure, I have seen anointed and gifted people hold back on our church; possibly because they were unhappy with my leadership style; perhaps seeing my limitations created challenges for them. The second example of *otser* is seen in churches who have resources, both economic and human, to plant new churches or send out workers but will not release them for the extension of the kingdom. They own property, have large buildings and great numbers of people but their vision and mission does not involve planting new churchs or sending workers, as a result, this is a barren womb. These individuals and churches "restrain" or "hold back" and are barren wombs.

A Dry Church

Lastly, **Tsiyah** (Isa. 41:18) means and speaks of being "parched and barren". It speaks of "a drought, a dry land and a wilderness". This last church body suffers from a case of spiritual dryness. Worship is dry, spiritual life is non-existent and a worldly, secular attitude prevails in this church. This can often happen as gifted people refuse to labour in the ministry, leaving a church to make do with available people. For a church to be progressive in the execution of its mission, it can't just be satisfied using anyone, no matter how available they are. They must be anointed because it is the anointing that destroys the yoke. When I was growing up in the church, I always heard "...God is not interested in skilled people..., He wants available people". I guess there is some merit in terms of uncovering someone's heart for ministry, but without the necessary skills, experience and anointing, availability alone can prove fatal. In the valley where David met Goliath, there were many available soldiers, even the King was available, however, this next move required more than availability. It required a God-approved ability. Recovery of a true spiritual vitality will change the atmosphere and can stimulate an authentic Apostolic move of the Spirit. This church must find a place of brokenness and weeping until the dryness breaks. Many things could have caused the dry state and only an authentic repentance and a deep yearning for the heart of God can remedy the dry hard condition.

As I close this brief section on barrenness in the church, let me offer you some advice that can break the spirit of barrenness in a church body. Here are four principles that you can apply to release the reproductive organ of your church and ministry. Remember, principles are only as good as the heart in which they are received. These principles are process developments that a body would need to rethink and seek the Lord about in order to see a revitalization of the womb. I offer very little techniques or tips, as they have too much potential to ignore your specific calling and context.

Four Principles

1. Churches and denominations should never transfer the responsibility of reproduction to someone else (e.g. a type of spiritual surrogate – where you look to others to do the work of church planting and reproduction). God's promise to your church is that He would multiply and bless the fruit of your womb. If for some reason you are unable to reproduce then align yourself with a ministry which is reproductive and support it with resources (e.g. financial, human and spiritual). For example, supporting a ministry can be prayer bands to pray specifically for a new church plant and for sending people on short-term mission trips.

2. Churches and denominations should open themselves to the prophetic word. God is constantly speaking about His desire for His church to grow and bring forth fruit. Be sensitive to God's voice. I would find it hard to believe that God is not speaking about your church's call to reach people. He has supplied His church with those with a prophetic ministry, and even in light of the perversion of this ministry in recent years, God still has

faithful and devote Prophets who do discern and know the mind of God for a specific season and situation. Prayerfully call on these people.

3. Churches and denominations must believe the word of God and allow those who He has given a word, to benefit the body. Groups that walk in fear will never do the faith-acts that produce fruit. To believe, is to act. Your ministry must seek a tangible way to be obedient to the call of God when a word is spoken.

4. Take the steps that produce fruit. Take active and deliberate moves to obey the great commission. Step out of the familiar and release your faith. Rekindle the fire of excitement, adventure, daring and risk. Send out young people, perhaps couples, who are willing to serve and plant new works. Two things must happen here. You must create a permission giving environment where young, and experienced people, feel safe to talk about what they believe God is doing in their lives. You, the leader should not be threatened by someone's desire to pastor, be a missionary or an evangelist. Secondly, you have to call them into ministry. Lay hands on them and tell them what you want them to pray about. In many churches, leaders expect potential candidates to instinctively, or of their own accord, come to them with a desire for ministry work. I had a young man in our church who I knew wanted to serve the Lord in ministry. I felt God was speaking to me about cultivating an environment of sending. An opportunity became available for ministry across the country. I called the young man and his fiancé into my office and asked them to pray and consider a term on the field. They prayed, came back to me and said yes, they would go. They were not yet married at the time but felt this was God. I think they trusted that I trusted them to seek God honestly, and they did and I believe God spoke to them.[33] Some leaders are afraid

---

[33] Mark and Jackie have been serving in British Columbia for just over three years now. At the time of the publication of this book they accepted the pastoral ministry of the church they have been serving in. They had the opportunity to return home, but they felt God calling them to remain and take over leadership.

of sending people, because if those people fail, it looks like God did not send them or speak to the leader. We have no guarantees with the outcomes of ministry, once we begin involving people in the work of the Lord; by the way, who are you to fear failing? Faith is a risky endeavour!

Think for a moment what Abraham and Sarah would have had to do to rekindle that fire in their tent in order to walk in their promise. As old as they were, they got busy because they believed God! As James put it, faith without works is dead.

Let me conclude by saying, inherent in the Great Commission are three key considerations to pay close attention to. These are the injunctions to, **"Go into", "all"** and **"the World".** Ed Stetzer in an excellent book, *Planting New Churches in a Post-Modern Age,* writes, "A church and denomination [for many this could read organization] can be mission-minded without being missional. It is always easier to *support* missions than to *be* missional." Jesus' call to us was to "go into". Our inability to act upon this charge is a telling depiction of our failure to obey Jesus at a very high and committed level[34]. Somewhere we lost the essence of what we are called to. Somewhere, many have lost the zeal for the growth of the church. Many of the fathers are to blame for not setting an expectation for further development of churches, but so are the children for not preparing themselves for a new ministry to a new generation or seeking God for His plan for their lives. The same spirit and attitude that was needed to flourish 30 years ago is the same spirit and attitude needed now. The power of the Holy Ghost, the zeal of the Lord, total sacrifice and a willingness to be obedient, are all vital traits. I am not asking if we should go. I am warning that if we don't go, it will mark the greatest decline of the Apostolic movement we have ever seen. This decline doesn't simply mean that churches will close, but something worse; the church will decline to its lowest common denominator and just survive for a few years with a

---

[34] I am a part of a group that at one time blazed a trail and planted many of the Apostolic churches we now attend or visit. What is a bit odd that the men that fathered us were themselves sent into the field as young men. Their fathers laid hands on them and sent them to plant churches, but somewhere over the years, they failed to commission young men, as they were once commissioned.

handful of people with no sense of purpose, while believing we are being the church. The commission does not suggest a casual, partial obedience. It demands a total commitment from anyone and everyone called a Christian. These words embody our apostolic heritage and they must be preserved at all costs. The best way to preserve the call is to engage it. Act on the promise of God. For those that are settled, they will be left behind. God is moving around the world with people who are hungry for more. Visit the movement of the worldwide Apostolic World Christian Fellowship[35] and see the millions who are contributing to the Gospel enterprise.

6. "One thing thou lackest..."

> *Then Jesus beholding him loved him, and said unto him,*
> ***One thing thou lackest**: go thy way, sell whatsoever thou*
> *hast, and give to the poor, and thou shalt have treasure*
> *in heaven: and come, take up the cross, and follow me.*
> (Mark 10:21)

Many of us want the better of two worlds when it comes to serving God. God, however, said that we cannot serve two masters, for either we will hate one and love the other, or we will love one and hate the other. It is difficult to love God and mammon, (often translated as money). The issue is not in possessing both but rather, the problem is in loving both. This rich young ruler was in his estimation faithful to his commitment to God. Coming to Jesus was a sincere attempt to find out how much needed to be done in order to possess eternal life. Jesus lovingly confirmed the obvious. Keep the law, and then sell all that you have, give to the poor and then come follow me. Jesus spoke to him on three levels. First, he needed to break his dependence on possessions; contribute to the welfare of those less fortunate; and become a disciple of Christ. This has always intrigued me because Jesus' command to this young lawyer was to *sell*, suggesting exchanging goods or services for a profit. I don't think Jesus was advocating him joining the ranks of the poor to be a disciple. Jesus

---

[35] www.awcf.org

was challenging him to part with the power that his possessions had over him. What he failed to see was that Jesus was teaching him that he was to serve others from what he had. The sale of his things would have returned a profit and with those profits he was to give to the poor, here he would be a disciple of Christ. Sadly, even that became too much for him because he was blinded by what he had and was unable to see the deeper reality of what Jesus was teaching.

For centuries, the church has advocated a poverty mentality in the execution and living out of the faith. Nowhere in Jesus' ministry does he denounce or decry the possession of wealth or riches. He does, however, decry the power that riches have on people. The church in this generation has swung the pendulum to the extreme, advocating a prosperity doctrine for all, with every believer needing riches to fulfill the Gospel endeavour. One only needs to visit some poverty stricken part of the world, and see extremely faithful Christians living for God, to turn that ideology on its head. In my missionary travels, I have seen poor Christians who are extremely faithful, whose commitment and service outshine those of wealthy Christians here at home. Poverty is not virtuous, but neither is wealth or riches. The key to our endeavour is the richness in our hearts that drives us to seek an abundant life in a personal relationship with Jesus Christ and the ensuing importance of reaching souls for the kingdom of God. One of the dangers that this text teaches us is that we must be careful in our ambition to be faithful to *our* religion and ignore *true* religion. Jesus called the rich young ruler to follow him and to serve others. Giving to the poor, and committing to serve, are marks of true religion (James 1:27).

7. "…we have forsaken everything to follow you…"

> *Then answered Peter and said unto him, Behold, we have forsaken all, and followed thee; what shall we have therefore? And Jesus said unto them, Verily I say unto you, That ye which have followed me, in the regeneration when the Son of man shall sit in the throne of his glory, ye also shall sit upon twelve thrones, judging the twelve tribes of Israel. And every one that hath forsaken houses, or brethren, or sisters,*

*or father, or mother, or wife, or children, or lands, for my
name's sake, shall receive an hundredfold, and shall inherit
everlasting life.* (Matt. 19:27-29).

Many of us make the decision to follow the Lord after we have heard
a soul stirring message, but it is not the response to the call that is the
greatest indicator of our character. It is our longevity, our ability to stay the
course. I believe it was normal for Peter to request some sense of assurance
after he had made such a sacrifice to follow the Lord. What is interesting
is that Jesus doesn't upbraid him for this kind of "what's in it for me"
attitude but, instead, shares with Peter and the others what the rewards is.
Jesus acknowledges the level of sacrifice people make to follow him, and
he assures them that it is not without pay or reward. Here is the point as
we examine Jesus' call to commitment. He says "For those of you who
have forsaken, abandoned, and cast off things in your life to follow me,
things like homes, familial relationship (e.g. brother, sister, mother, father
children etc.), possessions like real estate *for* my sake, you will be rewarded
for that kind of sacrifice, not just in the life to come but also in *this* life".
People have forsaken family for the pursuit of riches, and men and women
have forsaken their children for a new found relationship. Some have even
gone without basic necessities for long periods of time to attain riches. This
is not what Jesus says will be rewarding. It will be those sacrifices that are
made directly for following Jesus. You can lose your family for following
Jesus, you can lose land, and you can lose possessions, all for following
Jesus. Most of us do not want to consider this because it seems too radical,
too extreme, and yet, this is the kind of sacrifice Jesus may ask of us. We
are challenged to examine the Jesus we are following. Is he saying that we
have to arbitrarily and illogically abandon our families and possessions? I
don't think so! He is saying, however, that those who have made up their
minds to follow him, must follow with all their hearts, and that following
will cause people to make decisions that will affect every aspect of their life.
Consider this: many people who are coming to salvation among Muslims
must weigh the great cost of converting from Islam to Christianity. Often
times, decisions are made in secret or at the high cost of being disowned by
family and friends. That is not an easy decision to make; but the demand of

the cross, on the heart of someone who has come into contact with Jesus, convinces people to make those kind of commitments.

These seven commitments show us unequivocally that Jesus was not interested in halfhearted servants. He was not the "gentle Jesus meek and mild" that we often visualize. He was a fierce warrior, and a fanatical recruiter of deeply committed people. I have tried to find where Jesus spent time looking at people's track records to ensure that the new recruits were suitable for the tasks ahead. I haven't found any evidence of this. He wasn't looking for superstar Christians who had special talent and skills. He didn't have long meetings with a selection committee, he didn't conduct long interviews to assess behavior, but he did, however, challenge people to a higher, nobler call, irrespective of where they came from economically, socially or culturally. He spoke to the hidden treasures buried deep in people, desiring to find those who were ready and willing to access them.

As you read this, go back over the seven committments and give them a closer look. Ask yourself, what did Jesus really mean? What did the original audience understand about what he said? How have I applied these into my own life up to this point? Which of the seven commitments spoke to you the most? Why? Journal your thoughts and seek the face of God for his direction as you allow the word to shape your thinking and ministry.

CHAPTER 3

Paul, a Master Builder

Now let's look at Paul, the apostle, on building; a man we speak so much about and who I believe, we understand so little. Much has been written about his theology and teaching, for which we all owe a debt of gratitude; the basis of many of our fundamental principles and beliefs come from his pen. What many of us seem to miss is his work ethic, his ministry strategy and how he masterfully facilitated the spreading of the gospel throughout the Roman Empire. It should be noted that Paul was not the only Christian worker; there were other great workers who planted churches, who moved with zeal and passion to spread the Gospel to lands beyond. But, it is Paul whom the Lord saw fit to use to show us "the lay of the land", in terms of how we should work at extending the Kingdom. Paul was masterful in extrapolating the deep spiritual teachings of the Old Testament system of worship, but he brings us to a completely new level of worship, order, and ministry in the New Testament.

In 1 Corinthians 3, Paul referred to himself as a wise master builder, laying the foundation of the first apostolic, missional church. The character of the church was one of "intentional missionalism". With Paul's approach, and many other early worker's, the church was also incarnational, meaning that they were able to contextualize the Gospel in the places they were proclaiming the Good News. Ed Stetzer, masterfully outlines Paul's approach to the work of building the church. Paul was led by the Holy Spirit and in the execution of his ministry it wasn't only his theology that was inspired, but also his methods. We are beginning to understand why implementing the methods of the early church is such a difficult process for many of our modern day, established churches; it is because they are "established"[36] The church in the first century was not. It was an "emerging" great commission church. The genius in the embryonic DNA strand of the church Jesus was building throug Paul, was that the church was emerging and it was burgeoning. Established churches have too many challenges that hinder their ability to expand and grow in fresh ways that reach unchurched people in our culture. Established churches are able to attract people who are familiar with church life and practice. But, for the countless number of people in this generation, who neither understand or care to know what the church teaches, established churches have less success reaching them than, emerging great commission churches. Emerging great commission churches have a distinct opportunity to reach *new* segments of the culture. It should be noted that success is never guaranteed merely because of a method or structure. There are always multiple factors that contribute to the success of a budding or even, in some cases, established churches. Let's take a look at Paul's understanding, practice and methods in his master builder strategy.

1. Paul was personally prepared for his church planting ministry

- His world class formal training gave him a broad understanding of divine history
- He was vitally connected with God (2 Cor.12:7-9)
- He became prepared by stepping out in ministry from the start
- He was teachable; he apprenticed under Barnabas and he was willing to be under authority before God put him over others (Acts 11:25-26)
- He lived an exemplary life (1 Thess. 2)

---

36 The term "established" refers to a church which has gone through a full cycle of birth, growth, plateau, decline and eventually death. Once a church has reached the plateau stage its processes of growth has reached its limit. In order to avoid decline the church must intentionally reinvent itself in its methods, spirituality and purpose. An established church is usually 30 years or older, but can be younger chronologically depending on when it settles in terms of the churches culture.

2. Paul was an evangelist

- He began preaching right after his conversion (Acts 9:19-22)
- He was a *net* fisherman in two ways: he led entire family units to Christ (Acts 16:25-33), and he conducted large scale evangelistic meetings (Acts 13:44; 14:1; 19:9-10)
- He looked for those who were most receptive (Act 18:6)

3. Paul was an entrepreneurial leader

- He had a vision and call from God (Acts 9:15; Rom. 18:20-23)
- His vision and call was to the gentiles through leading missionary teams into *new territory* to plant churches. He combined "quick-strike" evangelism with church planting. The marriage of these two powerful methodologies sparked movements that made an impact for generations. (Many of our current organizational churches have begun to decline because they have lost their zeal for new territory. When the fire to start new churches in the early days was blazing, churches reached people. Once the church settled and developed an institutional mindset, the fire began to go out. The church became more interested in being established, (e.g. possessing buildings, either in buying or building edifices, having operational ministries, and hiring staff) than they were in continually expanding. There are many reasons for this, which we will discuss in full later, but one is worth noting here. Once a church becomes "established", it becomes more interested in size on one hand and stability on other. The church becomes focused on settling in one location instead of looking at the principles that Paul used to expand, a continual growth strategy through multiple locations. Maybe the church growth movement in recent years has convinced us that the mega church model is the ideal model to prove that a church is successful and God-called. I am not suggesting that the mega church model isn't relevant, but I am definitely saying it is not necessarily the ideal. I think the point here is that the church must seek to reach its maximum capacity

in any one location, while maintaining her zeal and fervor for expanding the overall Kingdom. To reach people, a ministry must consider its capacity to reach its maximum number of people without compromising the ideal of size; it is essential that we discuss growth and size, while at the same time develop a workable and sensible strategy for ongoing growth[37]).

- Paul selected the kinds of people he wanted on this team. He was not afraid to ask people to make sacrifices for the work and he was not afraid to deny people the opportunity to work with him, (Acts 16:2-3;15:38). In this process, he also appointed long-term leaders to the churches he started, (Acts 14:23). He gave direction where teammates should minister by delegating tasks to the field workers. I have seen, in my own organization, how this same process brought tremendous growth and expansion in the early years of the ministry, regionally, nationally and internationally. Many of the larger challenges that have surfaced in the past few years have come largely because of our inability to accept the fundamental principles discussed here, and how they contribute to the churches vitality and longevity.
- He received direction as to where he and his team should plant (Acts 16:6-10)
- He was a proactive strategist (Acts 13:14, 44-49). He established a reproducible pattern for his church planting program (Acts

---

[37] As I was reflecting on this point, I looked at the body with whom I am associated. Internationally headquartered in the U.K. and lead by what I call a modern day apostle, Bishop S. A. Dunn, I see the genius of bigness in an expanded incarnational and missional strategy. The church in the U.K. since its inception has expanded to some 50+ churches numbering well over 5000 people throughout the country. That is approximately 113 members per church. We know practically that some of these churches are small and some are large. In my conversations with Bishop Dunn, he was less interested in having a big church and more interested in sending and reaching people in different areas. Built into that was the desire to have a place for all the saints to worship together a few times within the year, so he spearheaded the building of a 5000 seat Convention Centre.

14:1, 17;2) and he deliberately did advanced planning (Acts 19:21)

4. Paul was a team player

- He was willing to be on a team (Acts 13:1-5)
- He always planted with a team (Acts 15:40;16:6;20:4)
- He had a "sending" base church which he reported to (Acts 14:26-28)

5. Paul was a flexible, risk-taking pioneer (1 Cor.9:19-21)

- He constantly penetrated new territory (Rom. 15:20)
- He targeted new groups (Rom. 11:1)
- He pioneered new methods of ministry (Acts 13)

6. Paul cared for people as a shepherd

- He invested personally in the lives of people (Acts 20;31)
- He was like a nursing mother and an encouraging father (1 Thess. 2:7-11)
- He was vitally concerned with the growth and development of converts (Acts14:22)
- He drew close to co-workers (2 Tim. 1:2)

7. Paul empowered others (Acts 16:1-3)

- In order to lead this rapidly growing movement, he risked delegation to young Christians.
- His team planted churches on their first missionary journey, and then a few months later came back to these new churches and appointed elders (Acts 13:13,21; 14:21-23).
- He recognized his own strengthens and weaknesses and delegated to others according to their strengths (Titus 1:5).

8. **Paul stayed committed to fulfilling God's calling and vision even at the cost of extreme personal sacrifice (Acts 14:19-20; 2 Cor.11:23-28).**

   - He never backed down, and he never gave up.
   - He maintained a thankful attitude in the face of cruel and unfair treatment (Acts 16:25).

9. **Paul was willing to let go of his plants and move on to plant more (Acts 16:40)**

   - It seems that Paul needed special encouragement to stay in a city for very long (Acts 18;9-11). The longest he ever stayed in any one place was three years (Acts 20:31). Ephesus was possibly his strongest plant and our best model (Acts 19:10)
   - He had faith in God's ability to keep the churches he started strong (Acts: 32)
   - He was willing to let his best teammates leave his team in order to benefit the kingdom of God (Acts 17:14)
   - He followed the example of Barnabas, who was willing to let go of the prominent leaders in the church at Antioch (Acts 13:1-4). [38]

What is important for us to understand from this list is that Paul had a particular mode of operation. It is important to decipher what that was and realize it is valuable today to how Jesus' will build the church. Without going into an extensive look at religious history, a cursory examination will serve us well. Paul and the other apostles ministered at a particular time in history when the Roman Empire was at her zenith. The church was an emerging entity with little formal structure. Its key to understand that church possessed without a "formal" structure. The structure in place did not hinder the mobility needed to spread quickly throughout the

---

[38] Ed Stetzer, writes this list to show how church planters should imitate Paul, the apostle, in the building and planting of new churches. I have used it to show the important elements of methods of emerging Great Commission churches and/or of churches that desire to re-develop themselves.

Empire. While there were leaders- the apostles contributed much to the new movement, much of the growth was facilitated by the larger Christian body- the believers. There were no buildings, but there were places to gather and fulfill the essential aspects of the fellowship and instruction. Although there were no dedicated church buildings, the church never stopped growing. I guess it is fair to say that they couldn't build and acquire buildings fast enough to manage the explosive growth the church was experiencing! I often wonder, if we were to change our attitude about buildings and focused on reaching as many people as possible, if we would reconsider how important buildings are.[39] Wouldn't it be awesome if we grew our churches so fast that building projects would get frustrated because we were reaching too many people? Imagine starting a new building project to build a 1000 seating capacity building, but, by the time you finish the project, your membership had grown to 2500 or more. The natural solution would likely be to have more than one service. I would agree with that strategy, but what if that growth came from people who moved away from the area, who evangelized new areas and desired to start pioneer works? How would you manage that? According to mainstream ministry philosophy and practices, we can't conceive this scenario. Many would see this possibility as divisive with the potential to destroy growth. Furthermore, we would see the pioneering venture as a gross interruption of the building project, as funds would likely be channeled away from the project.

The list above shows us how Paul managed people, and indirectly, we see the role of 'location' in the development of the ministry. There is not much emphasis on "place" in Paul's strategy, however, in our culture and after seventeen centuries(400A.D.–present) of Constantinian Christianity, we emphasize the growth of the church on the minimum number of

---

[39] It seems to me that buildings restrict our vision. We think as big as our buildings. So the basis of our vision is not the world, it is the capacity of our buildings.

people, the professional clergy, and the grandeur of a place of worship[40]. Let me reiterate, I am not suggesting not to have buildings. The issue is what a building has come to mean to us. Many ministers find their value and success more in a successful building project, than in a successful people project. However, if we keep our focus on people, we will no doubt have to deal with building projects. It's a matter of priority.

We now turn our attention to another kingdom builder, who I call the great door opener: Peter, the stone, the one with the keys. His role is unparalleled in many ways. Without him, the entire Gentile world would have been in limbo. The door had to be opened and our Lord chose Peter for that task. The Kingdom had come to birth and now it was time to deliver. The offspring would be a new entity, the church, composed of both Jew and Gentile, bond and free, barbarian and Greek.

---

[40] The focus on the clergy, as the people who know how to lead people to Christ, I believe to be one of the greatest misfortunes in the churches capacity to impact culture. I believe we have fostered a culture that explicitly teaches that the men and women who stand on the platform each week, are the ones who have knowledge and are able to lead the masses to Christ. So, inadvertently, believers best attempts at leading people to Christ gives rise to the second misfortune; believers are well equip to invite people to the place of worship, rarely ever able to instruct people on the principles and teachings of Jesus themselves. So what happens when the masses no longer are willing to come to the place of worship? The clergy have no one to convince, the trajectory of growth declines. Believers are ill equipped to minister to people who believe they are satisfied with life without Christ and the church. Church leadership must return to releasing people to do the *work* of the ministry.

CHAPTER 4

Peter and James on Building

*"And Jesus answered and said unto him, Blessed art thou, Simon Bar-jona: for flesh and blood hath not revealed it unto thee, but my Father which is in heaven. And I say also unto thee, That thou art Peter, and upon this rock **I will build my church;** and the gates of hell shall not prevail against it. And I will give unto thee the keys of the kingdom of heaven: and whatsoever thou shalt bind on earth shall be bound in heaven: and whatsoever thou shalt loose on earth shall be loosed in heaven". (Matt. 16:17-19)*

The role that Peter played in laying the foundation of the church is critical and extremely important for us today. Peter's contribution was essential and challenging. Jesus gave Peter the keys and the authority to access the kingdom of God; not merely for himself or any particular group of people, but Peter's ministry was going to change the course of history forever. Paul, in Ephesians, explains in further detail the far-reaching scope of this change when he taught on the universality of the church. He taught that the church is the body of Christ and it is comprised of people from *all nations, tongues, tribes, and peoples*. It is Peter; however, that gives us the first purview to this reality. In Acts 10 Peter is called to minister at the home of a Roman citizen in high authority. This man is a foreign ruler but he is also extremely sympathetic to the religion of the Jews. After receiving a dream from the Lord that he should send for Peter, he obeys and calls for Peter, who comes to his home. There, the apostle finds a house filled with Italians who are anticipating the news that Peter is to share with them. Peter begins to preach, the Holy Spirit descends in the room, and these Italians begin speaking with tongues. The Jews that accompany Peter are astonished that God has favoured the Gentiles by giving them the Holy Spirit. Without hesitation, Peter commands that these Gentiles be baptized in the name of Jesus Christ. The door is flung wide open and the Gentiles, who were without Christ, are now welcomed to be fellow-partakers with the saints and of the household of God (v19).

How was God using Peter in the building process? For many years, unfortunately, the church has emphasized only one dimension of this wonderful story, the coming of salvation to the Gentiles. I believe because of this, we have fallen into a sad state of missional bankruptcy and the church has lost its passion for mission. As the church in the Roman Empire had to grapple with the prospect of multi-cultural ministry, the Apostolic church of the 21st century must do the same. Peter and Paul reveal to us that the church now and then must be "middle-wall" breakers. The church must be willing and ready to confront the walls that separation and divide people from one another. This section of the book is not intended to deal with the deep implications of all the ethnic challenges in the church. We will address some of these issues later. The aim now is to highlight a critical element of Peter's ministry, a reality the church in the West must face head on. Peter would not have accomplished his calling without dealing with the issue of ministry beyond his cultural and ethnic ethos. Peter had to deal with several important things in the building of the church. He had to leave his current customs and ethnicity and minister to another group of people, despite his political, social and religious views. He had to confront his own inner battles, particularly his ethnic/cultural prejudices, to succeed with God in this endeavour; he had to understand the role and mission of the church; and finally he had to understand his role in the continuity of the Gospel, knowing when it was necessary to hand off to someone else, Paul in this case.

James on Building:

There are two important elements to an emerging great commission church. The first is leadership and, secondly, the church's ability to handle challenges and problems. The early church was so dynamic and vibrant that its growth created situations never dealt with previously. It was like a woman who is a new mother. Everything is new; every experience is a challenge to deal with, both good and bad. The church grew so rapidly, it had to confront problems as they surfaced. In Acts 15, the church was on fire, and defining the scope and parameters of management was out of control. The ethno-cultural issue, couched in a religious framework, caused the most problems. The apostles and the elders in the church in Jerusalem were not prepared to deal with the transformation that was taking place in the church. They settled on the church remaining within the establishment of Jewry. If there was going to be any "outsider" they would have to conform to Jewish legal codes like being circumcised and keeping the law. The first Council convened to address the issue of Gentile admittance into the church without having to keep the "law". This was a serious problem because earlier Peter had preached and baptized the entire house of Cornelius, and God had baptized them with the Holy Spirit. Paul and Barnabas had seen a great move of God among the Gentiles, many signs and miracles where done among them. They had planted congregations. The Gospel had spread as far as Ethiopia and showed no signs of slowing down.

After the controversy of the legalistic Jews, James gave the sentence. After carefully listening to the evidence presented by the apostolic band of emerging leaders, missionaries, evangelists, Paul and Barnabas and others, he does what is so vital for the church in dealing with important issues; he presents and addresses the situation in light of scripture. A proper understanding of what the church is obliged to do must be based in the Word of God, and that Word must find its relevance in contexts where people live. James could have done what most denominations and organizations' leaders do now: fight to perpetuate traditions or old knowledge that hinders a progressive move of God. But James was no status quo leader; he was compelled to shift, based on scriptural authority and the new evidence of God's hand at work among the Gentiles. He saw the church missionally, that it was God's intention from the beginning to bring the Gentiles into covenant relationship with Him. With this understanding, he throws the door open even wider, issuing the decision that the church now include the Gentiles. What is even more exciting is not only the inclusion of the Gentiles into the church, but, in order to keep expanding the church among gentiles, missionaries were needed. They recognize the immensity of the task and commission men to the work. They were not ordinary men, neither were they especially gifted; they were fiercely committed men, men who "... hazarded their lives for the name of our Lord Jesus Christ" (v26).

This calls to mind a story told to me about the difference between being involved and being committed. Some farm animals were having a discussion about who would be participating in an upcoming thanksgiving dinner. The Chicken boasted how involved she was because she was contributing eggs to the dinner. The cow boasted about how involved he was because he was providing milk, and the goat boasted that his milk was being used for cheese. However, the pig, silenced them all and reminded them that their involvement was nothing compared to his, he said "while you are all involved you are not committed. I am fully committed because I will be providing the bacon". The task of the missional church is not mere involvement; it calls for commitment. The men that went out were men that did not consider their lives dear to themselves, interestingly enough, they were not a rare breed in their day. I am afraid in many regions today, this kind of person is not easily found. James knew and understood that a missional church was not going to accomplish the vision of reaching the lost with just involved people, it called for committed people who do not count their lives more important than the call of God to serve.

James teaches us critical lessons on the church. These lessons focus on the role of leadership and problem solving in the early church, showing us how the church managed in the emerging years.

What is extremely interesting about the emerging Church of the first century is the dynamism that existed in the arena of culture. In Acts 6, the churches first real internal challenge came with the dispute over the treatment of one group in the church over another. This dispute is normative among those who seek a dynamic cross-cultural attitude to ministry development. I am sure, as some of you read this, you have an impression that this doesn't apply to you. Big mistake, it applies to all of us. To what degree it applies will vary, but we are all called and challenged to deal with people from different backgrounds and cultures. Those who live in a multi-cultural, multi-ethnic environment are more responsible and challenged to see to it that they contextualize the Gospel to their situation. It is a part of a missional mandate. Those who find themselves in a monocultural and monoethnic environment would do well to remember the great commission that obliges us to go to "all nations". None of us are excused from the call to the field.

The call of Jesus is a call to deep devotion to the purpose of the Kingdom. In this section, we tried to challenge you to see several important things about the church and Jesus' role in building it. The outstanding point is that Jesus calls us to a high level of commitment. He does not call whips, the fearful, cowards, the comfortable, or men-pleasers to his service. He calls those who are not afraid to toil when others sleep. He calls those who, at times, feel a deep inner inadequacy but move forward in spite of it; he calls those who are not afraid to lose all, to gain the riches of the life to come.

Where do you stand? When Jesus looks at you, what does he see? Are you willing to be challenged to become all that he desires of you, or, are you comfortable with how things are?

SECTION II

Incarnation vs Attraction

Who, being in the form of God, thought it not robbery to be equal with God: But made himself of no reputation, and took upon him the form of a servant, and was made in the likeness of men: And being found in fashion as a man, he humbled himself, and became obedient unto death, even the death of the cross. Phil 2:6-8

When I started researching the content for this chapter, I thought about the idea of mission, and of how people arrange their lives to accomplish their ends.

An Example from the Red Light District

Think of the career of prostitution. A prostitutes prime objective is to attract customers to patronize her or his enterprise. In order to be successful in this endeavor, they must become proficient in several things. Among other things they must know their audience well and they must have a good grasp of their territory, as it is frequently referred to in Real Estate, "location, location, location" is everything. They must know how to attract customers and, if effective, have them return for repeat business. Now, as they go on their shift, they must prepare themselves in a manner that will bring success. In the case of a female prostitute, she begins to adorn herself with particular clothing and certain perfumes in addition to applying lipstick and a variety of facial paints.

Everything about her is suggesting that she is attractive, we should note, attractive to a specific audience. Her entire enterprise hangs on her ability to attract people to herself. If she does not attract well, her enterprise will be negatively affected.

An Example from the Military - Delta Force

Now, on the other hand, think of a P.O.W (prisoner of war) in the deep jungles of an Asian rainforest that needs to be extracted from captivity. The rescue Delta Force must prepare themselves for the mission. They must know their task and be familiar with the terrain in which they will need to work. They too must adorn themselves in clothing that will allow success. They clad themselves with combats, matching specific colours with the terrain and their environment. They too paint their faces, but this is to disguise themselves and to be invisible to their enemies. This mission and enterprise is far more noble and important, but its success does not weigh on the ability of the task-force to be attractive; instead, it is in their ability to be imperceptible. Both endeavours seek to extract, they must go on mission, but both results do not carry the same value in the end.

Is it possible that the church, since the rise of Constantine, has operated in the attractional mode, much like the lady of the night? To be honest, there are many enterprises that operate in an attractional mode, so I am not suggesting that attractionalism is completely wrong; for examples, retail stores, schools, the entertainment industry, all operate in an attractional mode. I use this example to over-emphasize and to give you an extravagant mental picture of some of the dangers in operating in an attractional mode as a primary missional objective. Even if we were to use any of the less provocative examples, the point remains, attractionalism is an ineffective way to impact culture in the 21st century. In every way, the church's mission is far more analogous to the work of the Delta Force rescue mission. Unfortunately, the primary attitude that most Christians and Christian leaders have towards the work/mission of the church is attractional. I believe most well intentioned leaders desire an authentic approach to reaching lost people. Most pastors want to reach people with the wonderful Gospel message; however, many leaders have fallen susceptible to the idea of reaching people by any means necessary. Which leads to dumbing down the entire enterprise of the Kingdom. As much as we are to reach people, we must be mindful that the method and message of Jesus Christ, and the early apostles, are key elements to true Apostolic process and kingdom revival. Over the past three decades, the church has been bombarded by philosophies from the church growth movement. The semantics are deceptive; even though the phrase "church growth" seems innocent enough, the philosophies behind many are less than biblical. Let me be quick to add that not all church growth practices are bad or erroneous. What we are contending for here is an authentic Apostolic methodology. When we study the overall principles and practices of the church growth movement, it reveals that the very basis of the movement is based on attractionalism; which emphasizes, do whatever needs to be done to attract as many people into your church. Church attendance and the church's involvement in the community, fundamentally not bad things, become standards by which ministries are approved and considered successful. The speed at which we are able to get as many people to fill our buildings should not drive us, rather it is the degree to which we can make disciples for Jesus Christ that defines success in ministry. The early church knew nothing of these modern day methods. Modern day church growth techniques, based on attractionalism are so counter to the pattern of the early church, it is no wonder we seem to have lost our way[41]. Michael Penfold writes a compelling critique of the church growth movement and four startling problems that have deluded most Christian churches[42] on webtruth.org. Let me outline his points with some brief notes. I admit I agree with him, he hits the nail on the head when he writes,

"A majority of Western churches do not see a single addition through conversion in a typical year. So to try and turn things round many are rejecting traditional methods of evangelism and adopting a new 'church growth' model. Market research has convinced them that unbelievers stay away from church not because they reject Christ, but because they reject the church's boring presentation of Christ. There's no need to change the product – just the packaging – and the crowds will come flocking back."

It is important to be clear, what we are contending for is an authentic approach to doing the work of the ministry. I am not suggesting that singing from a hymn book is more worthy an approach to worship than

---

[41] When I mention "losing our way" I am speaking about the massive decline in attendance in North American churches over the past few decades. I watch as many of our churches continue to attempt to reach people but struggle and are frustrated as more people have little to no desire to attend church services. I hasten to say, it is not for lack of effort on the church's part. The challenge is far deeper, more complex, these reasons we will give more attention later, but suffice it to say that church growth techniques are, and can be, a poor attempt at solving a much bigger problem.

[42] http://www.webtruth.org/articles/church-issues-30/the-purpose-driven-church-(a-critique)-59.html

contemporary songs presented on a screen; neither do I want to suggest that casual dressing has less merit than "reverently suited congregations and preachers". Technically, I believe neither of these matter, as much as the need for a genuine seeking for the heart of God to accomplish His will in the earth. So, to a great extent, we have to give ourselves latitude not to be judgmental of any practice, but we do need to be discerning and watchful as to the spirit (motive and intentions), by which we do our business. Penfold gives us much to consider.

The first problem Pemfold identifies is the relatively recent development of the church growth movement (CGM) and its origins. He reveals that the origin of the movement began in the faulty concept of Robert Schuller, who believed himself to be the founder of the modern movement. In Schuller's own words, he declares, *"An undisputed fact is that I am the founder, really, of the church-growth movement in this country...I advocated and launched what has become known as the marketing approach in Christianity.... The secret of winning unchurched people into the church is really quite simple. Find out what would impress the nonchurched in your community [then give it to them]."* Herein, lays the danger of the philosophical underpinning of attractionalism. What has happened, very subtlety, is a gradual avoidance of the need for genuine repentance, sorrow for sin and the turning of the life to Jesus Christ. Schuller believed, "making people aware of their lost and sinful condition is the very worst thing a preacher can do". People must feel good about themselves and if you are able to accomplish that in getting them to your church, you are successful. Most churches are not aware that most of our modern strategies, infused in our evangelistic efforts, have their foundation on this very premise. I believe the more we seek to attract people to church who are seeking a feel good experience, based on what we marketed to them, they will eventually attend our churches on their own terms. When churches struggle to maintain standards of moral purity, holiness, and righteous, they are forced to sensor what is said in the church, so as not to hurt people's feelings.

The second problem identified by Penfold is the adoption of the business-church marriage. The principles that govern the business world are much different from the principles that govern the church and marrying the two can lead to a very unholy union. The assessment driven philosophy of qualifying church workers (based on personality and temperament) is a dangerous concept for Apostolic ministry. God has already determined that He will use base things to confound the wise. Penfold warns the church to compare Pauline methodology as in Acts 20 with this modern process. Paul mentions nothing about marketing, growing, and adopting. Instead, he warns the leaders to teach the whole counsel of God, watch for false teachers, and preach the pure Gospel.

The third problem Penfold identifies in the CGM is preaching positive needs - oriented sermons that entertain and amuse. The problem is that the message is created to address the "felt" needs of persons who are unconverted. This makes the Gospel a type of needs-meeting strategy to happiness. Churches that best position themselves as a needs-meeting ministry will see much more results in terms of bodies in the pews (seats), but not necessarily truly converted (saved) individuals. The danger, Penfold stresses, is "a total change in the techniques, style, and form of historical evangelical preaching that often twist scripture to make a point". Another aspect of this problem is the simple belief ideology of the sinner's prayer, a long denied concept in the Apostolic church. However, the idea that conversion can take place without conviction, repentance and a changed life, leads to a "just accept and receive" kind of faith and the job is done, which is unheard of in the New Testament. The Church Growth Movement teaches that to be right with God, one only need change or adjust their self-esteem.

The fourth and last problem Penfold identifies is the need of the CGM to adopt worldly approaches to the Gospel endeavour. "Whatever works" is the mantra and pragmatism is the goal. How do you attract people of the world to your church? You reorder your church to appeal to the world. The sinner is free to come in, but not with the notion that we are making the environment uncomfortable. The church need not borrow from the world to be effective.

At the core of this approach is the DNA of attractionalism: "Let's gather as many people as we can without discerning the spirit and checking sin at the door". Rick Warren classifies this as creating a crowd, and although there can be some legitimacy to having large groups of people attend a church, we must preserve the integrity of the authentic gospel, at all cost. We are not to encourage unbelievers having a half-baked experience by coming into a church environment that caters to their felt needs. We are however, to present the gospel of the life transforming power of Jesus Christ, initiated by people brought into an experience of genuine repentance. Therefore, attractionalism is a faulty proposition to effective church mission. J. MacArthur points out, "the notion that church meetings should be used to tantalize or attract non-Christians is a relatively recent development. Nothing like it is found in scripture; in fact, the apostle Paul spoke of unbelievers entering the assembly as an exceptional event not the norm (1 Cor. 14:23)". The assembly of believers is for edification, instruction, rebuke, reproof and doctrine. How do you rebuke and reprove if you have services with non-Christians in them? Personally, I have often felt the difficulty of this truism in ministry; this experience of the subtle pressure to censor what you say in the service, in case you offend someone who is unregenerate and not at the place to receive the Lord's correction. Whole movements spend the vast majority of their worship time trying to evangelize the lost that come to church buildings, feeding on the prevailing belief that people are saved at church. Pardon me for sounding repetitive, but seriously, look at what is happening around us. The postmodern world is not coming to our churches to be saved, as a matter of fact, they are not coming to our churches at all. On the flip side of this, we are ill equipped to venture out into the world to make disciples of all men. So what do we do? We work harder at being more attractive to the world, instead of going out and confronting them with the powerful Gospel of Christ. Attractionalism has a subtle and deceptive nature to it. It convinces us that we are impacting our culture. The vast majority of churches, that operate in attractional modes end up contending with worldliness. The unsaved are invited into our worship experience and subtly we adapt to accommodate them

The question we should be asking in the 21st is, "how did the early church reach the lost?" Great question! They embodied the spirit and understanding of incarnationalism, missionalism and true apostolicity. The church today must give itself to these elements to reach those without Christ. It is important to take some time to address the issue of where evangelism takes place: is it in church or outside of the church? The whole idea of attractionalism is to use the church meeting as the place where conversion takes place. I am persuaded that we have this wrong. In this era, it is essential that the saints immerse themselves into the fabric of the culture that is antagonistic, at best, towards it, and demonstrate the power of God through direct contact in the environments where we work, live, study etc. The scope of this book is not to give a detailed rationalization of this, but instead to give a keen examination of how religious and church history easily proves this.[43]

Let us look at the difference between a church that can contextualize the gospel to meet the current issues of the lost, without compromising biblical living and principles, and churches that are structured to attract people to a central place in order to meet God. Both models have the capacity to reach people, but that is not the main issue. The issue is the church's ability to be effective in a postmodern era. I believe we face a level of spiritual warfare unlike anything the church has seen in 17 centuries. We are quickly approaching the re-emergence of the Roman Empire's disdain of the Judeo-Christian existence. Some might even say its already here.

---

[43] The early church was born in a polytheistic world. The preaching of one God was a strange concept. People did not rush to a place to hear the Gospel messaged preached. For the first three centuries, the church had to stay in a very active missional mode, and the Spirit of God worked, confirming the work with signs. The conversion of Constantine caused the Christianization of the Empire and pagans, barbarians and many others flooded the 'church' - the state church. Great buildings were erected and people filed into these structures to hear the preaching. No one had to bring anyone with them as the entire culture and society was Christianized. This continued for hundreds of centuries until the age of Reason, the Enlightenment began to call into question the authority of the church and the Bible. In a strange way, this could have been God's way of purging the people from a system He had not given. People stopped coming to church and became secular. There was a cry for the separation of church and state. During this time, the church fought tooth and nail to keep its position of prominence with the people as the central institution for people to meet God. However, the crusades, the inquisition and the horror of the reformation and counter-reformation left its toll. The larger society wanted nothing to do with the church. The 'church' has managed to maintain some semblance of importance in the lives of people, but we are currently thrust back to the environment of the early church. This is where the mass number of people no longer seek out the church. The church must regain its early church missional drive to see the kind of growth and impact she desires.

In the first century, the church was clearly 'outside' of the world and the saints took the idea that people needed to be saved seriously; they went about without reservation or fear of their lives. They met with enormous disproval and lives were lost in great numbers; but something mystical happened - something wonderful. The bloodstains of the martyrs acted as fuel to the movement instead of extinguishing it. In diagram 1, you notice the world is outside of the inner circle, which represents the church. However, the arrows, representative of various worldly influences, are pressing into the church. As the world's system gains influence on the church, it begins to weaken the church's ability to fight off destructive viruses. Eventually, the church is unrecognizable, and I am not talking about anything external. The power of the Holy Spirit is absent as the lives of the saints are compromised; incarnationalism must become a fundamental and essential practice of our work in this period of history. The church must be radical and courageous, confronting and "casting down every imagination and every high thing that exalts itself against the knowledge of God, and bringing into captivity every thought to the obedience of Christ" (2 Corinthian 10:3-5). The church gains power when it moves in the spirit of missionalism: we don't react to the world, we take action and go. We take our doctrine into the universities and colleges. We bring it into the workforce, from factories to class rooms, retail stores and play fields, everywhere and anywhere. See diagram 2.

In the gospel of John chapter 4, there is a wonderful episode of the interaction between Jesus and a woman in a greatly compromised lifestyle. After a lengthy discourse with her, she realizes that Jesus was no ordinary man, she was convinced he was the Christ, the long awaited Messiah. It is her next act that reveals the inherent character of the gospel enterprise –"go and tell". Before there can be an invitation to the Lord, there must first be a "going", a "sending" that precipitates and carries the full weight and responsibility of the gospel message. She didn't casually stroll back into town with a half dead message. She ran into town, without regard for her reputation, her past or even the present fact she was living with a man. She commanded attention because of her encounter with the master. "Going and telling" is what I am referring to as the incarnational aspect of the ministry. This woman acted upon her town, needing no training, and not being commissioned. She went into her community (town) and shared her encounter with Jesus with the people. The "come and see" ministry model, what I am calling "Attractionalism" is a subsequent act of "going and telling". In our modern era, we have reversed the order and adjusted it to "come and see" and "tell". Very few "go". Moreover, for the ones who do go, they are usually on the evangelism team. Take some time and keenly look at our practices – we lead with attractionalism. Here are some of the huge assumption we make when we lead ministry with an attractional approach. We assume that most people in the culture are familiar with what happens in church. We assume that most people know about the gospel. We assume that most people want to come to church and learn about God; would you not agree that these are huge assumptions? We need to lead with incarnationalism.

I am convinced churches focus on attractionalism at the front end of their ministry strategy because it is easier, faster, relatively speaking, and less time consuming. People have to get involved in people lives with an incarnational approach. We have fostered a culture within the church where we just do not have the time or patience to do ministry incarnationally. Need I mention what we feel this will do to the economics of our operations? You see, big crowds mean more money, even if the attenders are not committed to Christ, the very fact that they show up to church means the ministry will see financial gain. I am not decrying the need for economic viability. However, when the offering plate motivates our strategies as one minister stated, we are going in the wrong direction.

In the next two chapters, we will discuss at greater length what incarnation is and how it applies to church ministry in this era.

Diagram 1

The Church in Maintenance Mode

Churches that are reactive and function in a redemptive capacity only, generally operate in an attractional, maintenance mode and thus the temptation to conform to people who enter the church. The church welcomes the community but fashions the services to accommodate without transformation.

Diagram 2

The church in Missional Mode

A church that operates in an AIM framework is a church that sees less infringement from the world as it acts upon its world, not the world acting upon it.

CHAPTER 5

The Incarnation

The incarnation is a fabulous theological truth that stands as the gateway of grace and truth. Without it, the mystery of salvation is shrouded under a cloud - a cloud that casts a dark shadow of hopelessness, despair and meaninglessness. The beauty of the incarnation is only partially realized as an individual experience. Its accumulative corporate significance is its real power. *What does the incarnation mean for us, the church?* Any church that will expose itself to the depth of that question stands at the doorway of meaning and purpose. Ultimately, this translates into a highway of hope over a valley of despair. This is the place where people are challenged to become a true disciple of Christ.

To incarnate is to 'become' like the thing to which you want to identify. It is to 'put on' the form or likeness of that thing. Therefore, the incarnation of Christ was the act of the eternal God 'becoming' like mankind. It is where God limited himself and put on the *likeness* of sinful flesh. God became a man, put on the likeness of sinful flesh, walked where we walked and felt what we feel. In our small human minds, we parade and postulate what we think his coming meant. So we take our human understanding and try to validate why we believe some men are better or greater than others. However, God did not come to be a white man or black man. He came as a human being. Incarnationalism is not likeness to external identifiers; it is in essence becoming like the "being" of a person. He identified with our personhood.

The theological implication of the incarnation is worth serious attention if we are going to fulfill our responsibility of being the church that God is building. There are several aspects of the incarnation we must understand. One is the *promise of the incarnation*. What does God say to us in the Old Testament with respect to His coming to redeem lost humanity? All the covenants in scripture come with promises, and, if correctly understood, we can live in a way that is extremely pleasing to God. Secondly, we must understand the *act of the incarnation*. What did He actually do in this great transaction that has so powerfully affected our lives and all humanity? Thirdly, what was the *price of the incarnation?* We have often taught that salvation is free, and yes, it is free for those who now come to receive it; however, there was a great price paid to offer it for "free". Lastly, what is the *outcome of the incarnation*, what does this act mean to us in the church today? How do we apply this concept to the work we do and the ministries we initiate and lead?

The Promise

> *"And the LORD God said unto the serpent, Because thou hast done this, thou art cursed above all cattle, and above every beast of the field; upon thy belly shalt thou go, and dust shalt thou eat all the days of thy life· And I will put enmity between thee and the woman, and between thy seed and her seed;* **it [the seed of the women] shall bruise thy head, and thou shalt bruise his heel"**. (Gen. 3:14-15)

We see the prophetic proclamation of the coming of the Messiah early in scripture. God had commissioned man, Adam and his wife Eve, with a divine injunction to manage the affairs of the garden. With that command are the stipulations of what is permissible and what is not. They are given the order not to eat of the tree of the knowledge of good and evil. Man can freely eat from anywhere except that one tree. Upon breaching that order, Adam and Eve, along with the entire human race are plunged into the ravages of sin and death. God must execute judgment and sequentially gives His sentence. It is in the verdict upon the serpent that we get a glimpse of one of the greatest biblical promises in all scripture. Not only does God judge the actual creature that allowed himself to be used by Satan, but he also judges Satan - the perpetrator, the one behind the entire scheme. Here we find our first promise of a savior, an incarnational promise fulfilled many centuries later. It is the promise that the "seed of the women" will "bruise the head of the serpent". This messianic promise speaks of the coming of a Deliverer, who would strike a mortal blow to the head of the serpent (Satan) and bring deliverance for all humanity. When the writer speaks of the "seed" of the women, he is speaking of a "man child." This was the act of Christ dying on Calvary's cross for the sins of the world. In order to do this, God had to robe himself in flesh (John 1:1,14; Phil. 2:6-8; Heb. 10:4-7). "Enfleshing"[44] Himself was the ultimate act of God to incarnate Himself to those He intended to identify with.

The next promise God made regarding His incarnation is in Isaiah 9:6-7.

> ***"For unto us a child is born, unto us a son is given:*** *and the government shall be upon his shoulder: and his name shall be called Wonderful, Counsellor, The mighty God, The everlasting Father, The Prince of Peace. Of the increase of his government and peace there shall be no end, upon the throne of David, and upon his kingdom, to order it, and to establish it with judgment and with justice from henceforth even forever. The zeal of the LORD of hosts will perform this."*

Here again is a messianic proclamation from the mouth of the eagle-eyed prophet, Isaiah. God shares with him the glorious truth of the character and authority of the messiah. Not only is He the promised savior, He is God who robed Himself in human form and is to be called "Wonderful, Counselor, The mighty God, The everlasting Father, and The prince of Peace. He is not "a" mighty God, everlasting father or prince of peace. He is "The", the only one. He is the all in all. How do we know Him? How did He make Himself known? He is **born** to us, He is **given**!

There are many more scriptures that highlight the promised incarnation of our Lord, however, these two should suffice to prove our point.

---

[44] "Enfleshing" is a term I use to describe the process whereby the eternal God embodies himself in a robe of flesh, a flesh body.

The Act of the Incarnation

In the act of the incarnation, we see what God actually did to enter the world. It is mind- blowing, majestic and baffling. It was an act of total sacrifice that the eternal God would humble himself, robe himself in flesh and come into a dying world. It is one thing to make a promise, but it is another thing to fulfill it. Sometimes making the promise is the easy part, but the difficulty is in mustering the courage and the integrity to follow through. In Philippians' 2:6-8, Paul explains to us what God did in this act of unselfish love.

> *"Who, being in the form of God, thought it not robbery to be equal with God:* ***But made himself of no reputation, and took upon him the form of a servant,*** *and was made in the likeness of men: And being found in fashion as a man,* ***he humbled himself, and became obedient unto death,*** *even the death of the cross".*

We see this act of incarnation in Christ's willing decision to take on all the limitations of man, and to identify so completely with him. He could not be a proper sacrifice without being able to relate to the feelings of humanity. The majesty of it all is that the eternal God "made himself..." and "...took upon him..." and finally, "...humbled himself and became...". Jesus Christ, the man. He was the same essence as the eternal; therefore, there was no need to consider any actions taken as robbery. He was the visible manifestation of the eternal. The only way we could see God was by manifestation. So, the act of fashioning himself in a human body was the single most important act that God could use to demonstrate the power of the incarnation for humanity. He came; He did not send anyone else to do that most noble of jobs. It was not a job that could be delegated to someone else. He deliberately and willfully chose to subject himself to the limitations of a body - a body that had all the restrictions of all mortal beings. He now could bleed, be hungry and suffer in ways that He had not before.

As the church (the body of Christ), the questions we must all ask ourselves is, "*how are we to act in relation to this great sacrifice and demonstration of love to the World? How can the church incarnate itself?"* If the church is to be truly Apostolic and missional it must be **incarnational.** Greatness is often preceded by a willingness to do whatever it takes to achieve an expected end. Our first responsibility is to see a world in dire need of the Good News. We must envision a great work of God in every region and then we must envision people responding to the word of God. Without this, no action will be taken. The church must willingly "make herself..." she must "...take upon her..." and finally she must "...humble herself and become..." a place where people find God; they come to her because she, like the Samaritan woman, goes first and compelled 'them to come'.

The Price of the Incarnation

> *"Who, being in the form of God, thought it not robbery to be equal with God: But made himself of no reputation, and took upon him **the form of a servant**, and was made in the likeness of men: And being found in fashion as a man, he **humbled himself**, and became **obedient unto death**, even the death of the cross". (Phil 2:6-8)*

For the price, we return to Paul's explanation in Philippians 2. Paul highlights three key elements in describing the cost, or the price, of the incarnation. The first is the price of becoming a *servant.* As noble as it is to serve, we cannot grasp this concept without understanding the deep sociological implication of servant–hood, especially in light of the position held by one who is a lord, a master. A lord or master is accustomed to being served. However, in the act of incarnation we see the transformation of a lord into a servant. This is a great price! In order to lift up man the Lord must first come down to a place where He can relate with all the feelings and affections of humanity. He cannot effectively do that as Lord, He must become a servant, a slave. He must become what men are; they are slaves, slaves to sin. Their master is Satan. It is this knowledge that moves the Lord to identify Himself with us. He subjects Himself to chains, the pain of humanity and the sting of sin. There is no other place where this act of servant-hood is more apparent than when we see Him rise from supper, kneel and wash the disciples' feet. He then says to them, "if I then, your Lord and Master, have washed your feet, ye also ought to wash one another's feet (John 13:14).

Second is the price of **humility**. This is one of the most misunderstood concepts in the church today. Frequently, what we see now is a strange arrogance, a kind of haughtiness that mimics humility. It is that manipulative spirit of wolves in sheep's clothing. The motivation to serve is not a deeply held value to contribute to the betterment of others, but driven by what the individual can get out of it. To some degree, it seems like the church has lost this essential element of her power.

The Hebrew word for humility is "Middah", which can be defined as "measure" and/or "a right place". Alan Morinis says, "without humility, either you will be so puffed up with arrogance you won't even see what really needs some work, or you will be so deflated and lacking in self-esteem that you will despair of being able to make the changes that are lit up so glaringly in your self-critical mind."[45] Humility is also the "limiting of oneself to an appropriate space while leaving room for others. Sitting in a predictable place, you make room for others to occupy their own "space"". The Talmud[46] tells a story of a Rabbi, whose humility caused the destruction of the Temple. The story records Rabbi Zechariah ben Avkulas, the ruling Rabbi at the time as the reason for a vicious attack on Jerusalem. "…a man named Bar Kamtza sought revenge on the Jewish leader of Jerusalem for offending him. He went to the Roman governors to inform them that the Jews were rebelling. To prove his point, he told the Romans to send a sacrifice to the Temple. Normally such a sacrifice would be offered up, but Bar Kamtza caused a minor blemish on the animal that was unnoticeable to the Romans, but that he knew the Temple priests

---

[45] Morinis, Alan. *Everyday Holiness: The Jewish Spiritual Path of Mussar* (Boston, Massachusetts Trumpeter Books, 2007)

[46] The Talmud is a collection of ancient rabbinic writings and is a fundamental source for Mussar teaching. The Talmud consist of two interrelated parts – the Mishnah, which is the text of the Oral Law (in Hebrew) and the Gemara (written in Aramaic), which is a commentary and exploration of the Mishnah. The Talmud exists in two forms: one known as the Babylonian Talmud and the other as the Jerusalem Talmud, both of which were compiled and redacted between 200 – 500 C.E.; Everyday Holiness, pg. 299

Alan Todd

would see. Since a sacrifice must be without blemish, Bar Kamtza knew that the priest would be bound to refuse the offering. This refusal would be the proof that the Jews were in rebellion against Rome."

When the sacrifice came before the priest in the Temple, they immediately spotted the hidden blemish, as Bar Kamtza knew they would. What he may not have anticipated was that they immediately understood what was going on. Someone suggested that they go ahead and offer the sacrifice anyway. Rabbi Zechariah ben Avkulas, however, argued that if they did that, people would draw the incorrect conclusion that it was permitted to offer blemished sacrifices. It was then suggested that Bar Kamtza be killed to prevent him from telling the Romans and endangering the Jewish people. Rabbi Zachariah ben Avkulas responded, saying, "if we do so, people will incorrectly think that those who inflict blemishes on sacrifices are to be put to death." As a result of the priest's unwillingness to accept either course of action, Ben Kamtza succeeded in his plan. The sacrifice was denied and as Bar Kamtza had planned, the Romans took this to mean that the Jews were in rebellion. The Romans attacked and ultimately destroyed the Temple. The Talmud concludes, "the humility of Rabbi Zachariah ben Avkulas caused the loss of our homes, the burning of our sanctuary, and our exile from the land."

The conclusion is that the Rabbi showed humility by not acting presumptuously; but, he showed too much humility, because he shrank from the task he had been handed. His had a flowed sense of self, unable to believe he was capable of solving a real-life dilemma of great consequence. The story teaches that an inappropriate measure of humility is neither virtuous nor commendable. "Too little humility – what we'd call arrogance or conceit is easily seen as this sort of spiritual impediment". Scripture teaches that "The arrogant cannot stand in Your presence; You hate all who do wrong"[47] (Psalms 5:5). What we are to pursue is this noble cause of humility. Proper humility means having the right relationship to self, giving self-neither too big nor too small a role in your life.[48] When we get a proper handle on humility, there will be a divine release of the power of God upon the people of God, the church.

---

[47] The Hebrew version of the Old Testament

[48] Everyday Holiness, pg. 53

104

Lastly, we have the price of **obedience.** Paul teaches us that *Christ became obedient unto death.* It wasn't just any death, but the horrible execution of the Roman cross. He was keenly aware that the price of incarnation would cost him the deliberate submission of his will to the will of God. He said "not my will, but thine will be done…." (Luke 22:42). He was speaking of his acceptance to offer himself up as a sacrifice for the sins of the world. Christ submitted himself and followed the orders commanded from the Father, dying for the sin of the people satisfied the anger of God against sin.

Bishop S.A. Dunn once preached *"I've been robbed!"* The church has been robbed! She has lost these great virtues of servant-hood, humility and obedience. Now we are struggling to resist the tide of self-exaltation, arrogance and self-will. Ironically, if she regains the virtues, she will regain and revive the great anointing needed to propel her to influence a culture void of any power to find God.

Finally, there is the result of the incarnation.

The Result of the Incarnation

> *Therefore, God elevated him to the place of highest honor and gave him the name above all other names, that at the name of Jesus every knee should bow, in heaven and on earth and under the earth, and every tongue declare that Jesus Christ is Lord, to the glory of God the Father.* Phil 2:9-11

On the account of Christ's willingness to pay the price, Paul teaches that the outcome of the incarnation is impartation of divine favour. Christ was a recipient of the full disclosure of divine power. His willingness to lay down his life as a humble and obedient servant, afforded him all the power heaven had to offer. By his own admission, Christ rose and confessed, "all power was given unto him in heaven and earth" (Matthew 28:18). That power was resident in his name and authority. Paul says, "Wherefore, God highly exalted him and gave him a name which is above every name…" (Phil 2:9-10). The entire platform of the incarnation points us to the resurrection; there could be no resurrection without the incarnation. In other words, he could not overcome death without first becoming human. He had to "come" before he could overcome. The incarnation was to the resurrection what John the Baptist was to Jesus Christ. The former came to lead the way to the latter. In a wonderful way, we see the magnanimous love of God. It was because of his great love for us that he came to us, and it was that same love for us why he willing died for us. God has sandwiched us right between his two great acts of love and it is incomparable to anything we could ever fathom.

I propose to you that the Apostolic church must be an incarnational entity if she is really going to be who she is called to be. Since Jesus is the head of the church, when He promised that He would come, He was ultimately promising that the church was that promised place where humanity would find peace, relationship, counsel, and hope. She is a beautiful promised city set on the hill that "cannot be hid". She is the salt of the earth, and she is the light of world. However, she must also act courageously, valiantly, willing to lay her life on the line for the lost. The early church understood this, so it was common to find men that "hazard their lives for the cause of the Gospel" (Acts 15:26). The church must be willing to pay the price to glorify God. This can only be done by fulfilling the mind of Christ (Phil. 2:5). The church must become slaves to the will of the Father and be willing to do whatever God desires. To accomplish this, she must humble herself and be true to her calling. The church must be willing to lay down everything, take up the cross, and follow the Spirit. When a church does these things, not as some mechanical process but more as an organic metabolic process[49], she will receive of the Father the power necessary to be who she is destined to be.

---

[49] The idea of *organic metabolic process* is a scientific term that refers to the sum of the physical and chemical processes in an organism by which its material substance is produced, maintained, and destroyed, and by which energy is made available. The church is not a machine, it is a living organism. Our modern church practices seem to thrust upon us unnatural practices that are artificial and contrary to natural life system growth. A machine can function systematically, but it cannot grow. Living systems operate like mechanic systems but have a unique advantage, they grow. The one similarity that both mechanic and living systems share is there capacity to allow efficiencies; we must strive to find those very natural processes, therefore, I am proposing that we replicate living system in our practice of ministry.

CHAPTER 6

The Incarnation and Church Ministry

Can the church 'enflesh' herself? Can She find her natural capacity as an organism that carries life? The questions are a bit odd, but if the spirit of Christ is operating in her, she will naturally find ways of 'becoming all things to all men'. This is a very complex issue. I would like to offer some suggestions, however, for how the church can live out the incarnation. Please note that I am not making any attempt to lay out any technique or model. Instead, I offer you suggestions as to how to we can think about what needs to happen in our varying situations and contexts.

RE-thinking Discipleship

Churches must think deeply about what God's original intent is for the church. I believe God showed us what that is from the beginning. It is in Genesis 1 that "God moved on the face of the deep", as a response to the earth being without form and void. The church must "move" upon the face of the world, where there is chaos and hopelessness. This cannot be dealt with by some neat program and activity in our ministry calendar year; instead, we must teach the saints to think and act as God does. For many churches, the willingness to re-evaluate their discipleship process is something that carries very little interest. Sadly, this is the reason many people will be lost at the end of time. The church is too comfortable doing things the way we always have. Re-educating saints is too much work.

I have to admit as a pastor, I have felt the stress of attempting to reframe the minds of saints that have been in an attractional mode of operation for decades. Dismantling old systems, at times, seems very unsettling. However, if the cause of reaching the lost, especially those outside of our primary cultural ethos and context, outweighs our allegiance to an antiquated system of trying to attract people to our church buildings, then the stress is worth it. Before you get ready to attack me, familiarize yourself with the statistics in North America or even the Western Hemisphere. The number of people who have stopped going to church, our places of worship, but who are still seeking after God may surprise you. Rebecca Barnes and Lindy Lowry wrote a compelling article, *7 Startling Facts: An Up Close Look at Church Attendance in America* that states less than 20% of Americans regularly attend church, half the number of the pollsters report. The numbers in Europe are even worse.[50]

Proceeding with ministry under the same old processes without rethinking its value and worth is, frankly, unwise. Our teaching must lead people to a new way of thinking about the ministry, and what needs to happen to reach this culture and generation. It is important to note that things that worked decades ago, although necessary and effective for that generation, cannot be simply recycled with new language or little tweaks. Instead, we must find an entirely new language, attitude, and process for carrying out the mission of the church. What I am saying may seem a bit conflicting because, ultimately, I am advocating re-discovering the processes of the first century church (the early church). The elements of this generation and culture is almost a mirror image of that of the first century church's. What worked in the first century will work now and better due to our advantages i.e., the internet, transportation, and a host of other forms of communication that make reaching people with critical information easier and more accessible. The Apostolic church has a transcendent message that is not limited by time or space; it is applicable to all cultures, people and languages. The message cannot change, for it is the message that saves, but the execution of the message can find new and endearing

---

[50] *http://viaintegra.wordpress.com/european-church-attendance/*

ways to reach people. I am advocating a return to the original methods used by the apostles. Barnes and Lowry's research shows, and proves, that the early strategies employed by the early church are becoming commonplace with groups looking to have the results the early church had.

RE-lease the People

The church must examine its attitudes and beliefs about people, especially in terms of ministry, teaching, and soul-winning. I am 100% persuaded that one of the biggest reasons churches do not experience exponential growth, is because we attempt to reach the largest number of people with the fewest number of people. In other words, we hope to fill our building with prospective Christians, via the service of a few people, the clergy, those we classify as the experts who must persuade people to commit their life to Christ. Unfortunately, this is usually the extent of the ministry called "evangelism" in most of our churches. Imagine what could happen if we changed this and the largest number of people were released to reached the largest possible number of people? The saints, members in churches would all participate in the transformation of people who do not have a personal relationship with the Lord. Consequently, what would happen if they all worked at persuading these prospective Christians in giving their lives to Christ? This is what I am calling missional-incarnationalism [M-I]. Do not go to the bank with that term. Call it whatever you want. The point is that every believer can engage people in their sphere of influence, reaching individuals where they are and, ultimately, winning them into the body of Christ.

You might ask, how is M-I different from evangelism? There are small, yet significant differences. With M-I, each believer (disciple) would incarnate themselves, giving birth to so many occasions to touch people, it couldn't be controlled. People would be surrendering their lives every day and everywhere. Evangelism, as we know it, is a patented church program that only a few people participate in.. In some quarters, churches have been successful in enlisting large numbers of a congregation to participate in evangelism. This is not all bad, it is just limiting in its ability to explode and extensively reach a lost and dying world. Now, give this serious thought, because this is where most established churches, entrenched in a maintenance-attractional mode, hinder their development. Consider the possibilities of this kind of operation.

If you feel uncomfortable and are anticipating difficulties with the idea of an M-I model to ministry, this is an indication that you have to evaluate your belief about the potential in people. Most people live up to the expectations significant people in their lives have of them, i.e., parents, teachers, leaders, preachers, spouses etc. Having good and positive expectations of people will release *us* to believe in their potential. If given the right environment and support, people will exceed our expectations of them, and the Lord will add to the church daily, such as should be saved (Act 2:47).

RE-thinking and RE-organizing Leadership: Are we doing things right?

There are some leadership issues necessary for the functioning of an Apostolic ministry that warrant our attention. These issues may be the most critical of all. Rethinking leadership will call for something far more endearing than the latest leadership philosophy. The quality of leadership determines the direction the church will take. If leaders decide to commit to a biblical example of leadership, the church will experience a God ordained move of the Spirit and eventually will affect many people. However, if leaders decide to adapt to the latest trends or fads, the church may experience some growth, but will eventually experience the fate of many other churches through the ages. It will become a decaying, mediocre religious system or, even worse a false religious system that looks like the church of Christ, but at its heart it's something much less. Unfortunately, many churches are headed in this direction, as they build their ministries around the personality of the pastor.

The interesting thing is, the sovereign God can, and will, continue to bless in spite of the processes we use. For instance, in Philippians, Paul wrote that "some indeed preach Christ even of envy and strife and some also of good will; the one preach Christ of contention, not sincerely, supposing to add affliction to my bonds…" (Phil 1:15-16) Paul knew that God was ultimately in charge of the outcomes of the church. What I am contending for, however, is not just success of any kind. We should be seeking the kind of activity and success the early church saw. Not just in its dynamic and expressive displays of the Spirit, but in its methods of operation. Those methods stimulate a fast moving, culture confronting, expanding kingdom. Later in the book, I talk about the clergy-laity divide that has become the standard form of leadership and saint-hood in the church, but for now let's look at some other key issues.

There are some very challenging issues to discuss and I hope I can provoke your thinking in this area. We must see and understand the need and value of true biblical leadership in the church. At the same time, we must be careful not to let the 'idea' of leadership become the main focus. It seems to me that, in our generation, there is almost a cultic attitude towards leadership. Author John Piper writes in *Brothers, We are not Professionals* a riveting reminder to leaders of their proper place in the Body of Christ. We are not executives; we are not lords over God's heritage. Church leaders are **servants.** Many of the modern gurus on leadership seem to be selling us a "strange fire[51]" concept of leadership, the "executive" kind, and not the "servant" kind. Many pastors and leaders are more comfortable being called Chief Executive Officers, and the like. Jesus teaches the difference between worldly leadership models and Kingdom leadership. We would do good to align ourselves with Jesus' concept. This is not to suggest that there are not valuable lessons, antidotes, strategies and principles that can't be utilized from corporate business, not-for-profit organizations, agencies and governments. We just have to be very careful when we are crossing lines that will disrupt the spirit of the church. Allow me to repeat, this may be the most critical and challenging section of this book. I realize that much of what we do, and have accepted, in our leadership structures are unscriptural and based strongly on the traditions of men. These traditions, however, have become so entrenched in our psyche that

---

[51] I use this term because there is no doubt that leadership carries the force of fire, inspiration, and influence, but when those elements come from another source other than the Holy Spirit in the church, this is strange fire. Godly leadership should emanate from the heart of God into His chosen vessels.

they appear scriptural and true. What is required is a return to scriptural authority as the basis of our ministry operations, church government and polity. The challenge is how to reverse centuries of systemic error in methodology and practice.

To those of you who are concerned about a true biblical practice, I hope I can clearly present the errors, the reasons for these errors and possible solutions, to allow the church to return to her original form. The prospect of the church living out her true mandate is exhilarating; but it is not a simple or easy process. It will require you to grapple with the maniacal grip of tradition; traditions that have crept into the practice of the church. These traditions are not scriptural and have little, to no, theological support for their existence in the church. I am going to trace and weave together some key elements where, I believe, we have gone terribly wrong. Here are the unscriptural practices I will address: 1. The Monarchial Bishop or one-man pastoral system; 2. the absence of the plurality of elders, 3. the dysfunction of the five-fold ministries and finally 4, the dependence on titular authority, authority invested in names and titles.

Each of these areas deserve attention. However, as stated earlier, our main intention must be to dismantle ideas and practices based on men's traditions, and embrace a deep, passionate commitment to biblical truth and purity. Anything else leaves us suspect of making God's word and work null and void. The apostle Mark recorded Jesus as stating, in his harsh rebuke of the Pharisees and Scribes, that they taught the traditions of men as if they were doctrines and commandments from God (Mark 7:1-13). Blindly, many of us have not stopped long enough to examine how true this is in our practice of church leadership. We teach and practice things of men as if they are precepts of God, not realizing that this has greatly hindered the work and move of the Holy Spirit in His church.

Let's address the most familiar and accepted practices of leadership and church government by examining them through scripture. I must honestly say that this is as much a challenge to me as it will be to many of you reading. I too must grapple with the revelation of church order and structure, and wrestle to align myself with the word of God.

The One-man Pastoral System

Why has the one-man pastoral system[52] been the prominent model and practice of church government? Is it biblical? Was this the practice of the apostles; is this how they set up the church? Kevin Conner,[53] in his exhaustive work on the New Testament church, records that the one-man pastoral system has no biblical basis. He states "there is not one New Testament church among 48 churches (house church or otherwise) seen in scripture that had the traditional "pastor" or one-man over it system". This is a bold statement; one I wrestled with. The statements made about the seven churches of Asia, in the second and third chapters of Revelations, where John writes, "Unto the angel of the church of…Ephesus, Smyrna, Pergamos, Thyatira, Sardis, Philadelphia and Laodicea", came to mind first. Seven stars, which the Lord reveals to John, are the seven angels to the churches (Rev. 1:20). Surely, this is a picture of a one-man set up! Then I discovered that the word "angel" means "messenger" and does not definitively refer to a 'pastor'. What's more, I began reflecting on the congregational set-up in the first century when these letters were distributed; no single-building church where all the saints in a city gathered weekly existed. The saints gathered in houses (house-churches), rented halls, and outside in courtyards (Acts 2:42-46). Marvin Arnold[54] estimated that, in Asia, there were hundreds of thousands of believers by the end of second and third century. It is also important to note that there were no mega churches or ministries at that time, as we have today. Gatherings were scattered throughout cities, towns and hamlets. So, when John writes "…to the angel of the churches" who

---

[52] Let me clarify, I am not attacking the concept of the one-man pastoral system to be brutal or mean. I, like many who will read this book, are more than likely in the role of the one-man pastorate. This is because we have evil or bad intentions, but simply because we have never really stopped to think about it. We just accepted things at face value. However, we are committed to seeking the truth and then walking in it. My observations are an attempt to point the church to a biblical methodology that will uncover long forgotten truths of the power of the church.

[53] Conner, Kevin. *The Church in the New Testament*. City Bible Publishing. Portland, Oregon. 1982

[54] Arnold, Marvin, Christian Church History: Vol. 1, Arno Publishing, Washington, Michigan. 1987

was he addressing? The angel or "angelos" was an overseer and or elder, not a single, one-man pastor in isolation to other serving leaders. We will see this later, but the pastor is not the only messenger; Phillip was a "messenger", an "angelos" to Samaria, but his office was that of apostle-evangelist.

The New Testament does not record the term "pastor" when referring to any particular individual. We cannot find the idea of the pastor as the head or leader of a church assembly in the Bible, but today it is considered the norm. The pastor is the first person thought of when referring to a church body. Why? In 1 Corinthians 12:27-29, Paul lays out God's architectural design of the church when he said that God has set first in the church "apostles", secondly "prophets", thirdly, "teachers....". Yet you rarely hear anyone called "teacher" unless they are a part of Sunday school. Paul doesn't even add pastors to this list to the Corinthians[55].

Don't miss the point here; I am not saying the Bible does not mention pastors or the role they play in the church. What I am presenting here is how the term is used in the scriptures. The church world, Christendom, has completely misapplied the term and its proper function in the church of God. Therefore, we must re-think this and order ourselves correctly to see the intended results and revival in our churches. To add to this un-scriptural application, think about this: the office of the pastor, listed in Ephesian 4:11, is one of the five-fold ministry roles. The pastor, listed fourth, is combined with the teacher. Why do so many churches hesitate to call people "apostles", "prophets" or "evangelists" and "teachers"? Why is the "pastor" the venerated office and position that assumes all the attention, influence, and importance in the church leadership structure? Why do we look at the other five fold offices with such disdain, suspicion and criticism? For this reason, many men and women believe they have to be pastors to serve or function in the church. I have seen gifted and called missionaries, evangelists, and deacons fight to enter the pastorate. Sadly, they thought that the pastorate office would validate their calling and worth to the ministry and kingdom of God.

Even worse, churches have split because the one-man system creates a bottleneck causing undue pressure on the ministry. Gifts are stymied and before long there is a rupture, the church splits, people are wounded,

---

[55] In his epistle to the Ephesians Paul does add the term "Pastor" to the list commonly called the five-fold ministry (Eph.4:11).

leaders are left bitter and entire churches are devastated. Ultimately, gifts are suppressed under the one-man system. The most pathetic outcome in these situations is when the gifted are suppressed but they do not leave the church. Either they sit in silent frustration and bitterness, or they become the source of internal strife and conflict. Gifted leaders become passive and indifferent to any condition that may creep into the church. Both these conditions greatly hinders the church.

Let's turn our attention for a minute to the person in the seat of the pastor. I remember seeing my first job description of a local church pastor and wondering silently to myself "what have I gotten myself into...is this possible?" Pastors are expected to be all things to all people: satisfy everyone, upset no one, chair meetings, visit the shut-in, conduct one-on-one Bible studies. Not to mention, the important, and sacred job of preaching the gospel. It is no wonder so many pastors are leaving the ministry today. I know some of you are tempted to say "they were never called", but be careful; look closely at your situation, if you are a church leader, I am certain there are several tasks you have had to delegate, drop or just avoid to keep your sanity, marriage and family in good shape. The pastor is expected to carry an unrealistic burden for the church, at least in our modern practice. We are misled to believe that this is an acceptable practice because of the relative success of many single pastor churches. However, let me remind you that the vast majority of churches in the West have congregations of no more than 100 people. The average is closer to 50 people, which should cause us to rethink what success really looks like. The few churches that bolster numbers in the hundreds are few, and the ones with thousands are even fewer.

Where did the one-man system come from? The culprit is a spirit Jesus warned against. Mark, Matthew and Luke all record Jesus' warnings, Mark records,

> *"But Jesus called them to him, and saith unto them, Ye know that they which are accounted to rule over the Gentiles exercise lordship over them; and their great ones exercise authority upon them. But so shall it not be among you: but whosoever will be great among you, shall be your minister: And whosoever of you will be the chiefest, shall be servant of all. For even the Son of man came not to be ministered unto, but to minister, and to give his life a ransom for many".* (Mark 10:42-45)

Matthew records his account:

> *"But Jesus called them unto him, and said, Ye know that the princes of the Gentiles exercise dominion over them, and they that are great exercise authority upon them. But it shall not be so among you: but whosoever will be great among you, let him be your minister; And whosoever will be chief among you, let him be your servant: Even as the Son of man came not to be ministered unto, but to minister, and to give his life a ransom for many"* (Matthew 20:25-28)

Finally, Luke records:

> *"And there was also a strife among them, which of them should be accounted the greatest. And he said unto them, The kings of the Gentiles exercise lordship over them; and they that exercise authority upon them are called benefactors. But ye shall not be so: but he that is greatest among you, let him be as the younger; and he that is chief, as he that doth serve. For whether is greater, he that sitteth at meat, or he that serveth? is not he that sitteth at meat? but I am among you as he that serveth."* (Luke 22:24-27)

These are three New Testament witnesses. A spirit rose its head up in the Monarchial Bishop system, the lording over God's heritage. It is the position and spirit of control and suppression. We see it negatively manifested in Diotrephes who, John wrote, "... loved to have the preeminence among them, and received us not" (3 John 9, 10). From the New Testament, text we see this spirit in its formative stages gaining traction and slowly developing into a hierarchical system that created ascending ranks among gifts and offices; not for functioning purposes, but for self-aggrandizement, importance and influence. Somehow, the office of the pastor became the ruling office in the church: the dominant leader who presided over the affairs of the church. Over the centuries, the pastor's role has become predominantly administrative and less nurturing – which is the original meaning for "poimean" (shepherd). This is the root of the issue, but it took centuries to entrench the philosophical and theoretical elements of the office into its modern day reality. We all bought into it; hook, line and sinker. Somehow, we drank from the same cup of the false church, mentioned in the book of Revelations. The church borrowed many practices from the world system, particularly its attitude on the role of leadership. The spirit that presides now is the same spirit Jesus spoke of. I do not think there is a denominational group that has avoided this conundrum.

Is there another way? Does the word of God give us a more endearing way to practice church leadership? Yes.

The Set-Man and Shared Leadership: The Biblical Model

Now, does all this mean there shouldn't be a point leader in the composition of the church? Absolutely not! Leadership in the kingdom is necessary. What we see in scripture is a shared leadership model, with a point leader. This point leader bears the designation of a "set-man", a "chief speaker" that acts in the front role. This may seem like a contradiction to all that has been said up to this point, but let's look closer at the distinctions. In Numbers 27:15-27, Moses makes a request of God to "set a man over the congregation…" This leader was to go out before them [the people], to lead them, to direct them, so that they would not be shepherd less. God approves of Moses' request and designates Joshua to be the "set man". He brings him before Eleazar the priest, and the people. He was consecrated and charged before them all.

The first reading of this scene may cause you to believe that Joshua was a one-man pastoral leader, but he wasn't. Let us go back to Exodus 18. Moses delivered the children of Israel out of Egyptian slavery and then camps out at Mount Sinai. Jethro, Moses' father-in-law, joins Moses and reunites him with his wife and children. After rejoicing for the victory of the Lord against Egypt, Jethro witnesses Moses operating in a one-man pastoral system. He stood from morning to night judging the matters of all the people. Jethro asked Moses, what he was doing (to the people), and why was he doing this "alone"?

Now, Moses' response reveals that he was ignorant, foolish or perhaps just arrogant. Moses seemed to believe he was solely responsible for judging the people. I believe Moses was ignorant. He didn't know better; therefore, he needed counsel and instruction on leadership, management and organizational development. Jethro's counsel to Moses, I believe, reveals how leadership should be conducted in the Kingdom of God. Moses' job as an "apostle" was to instruct and teach the people how to obey God and live before him. His ministry was "the word" and "prayer". The pastoral ministry needed to be off-loaded to others who met specific qualifications and had a certain capacity for leadership. Moses was to share leadership by appointing other men who were able, skillful, proficient, reverent, honourable, men of integrity, men of truth, honesty and righteous, men who hated covetousness, men of character who could not be bought, and were not greedy for things; and finally they had to be able to lead the people. These men had to have the leadership capacity at varying levels – some able to manage 1000 men, others hundreds, others fifties, and some tens. The key is they were to *share* the leadership with Moses. Therefore, Moses was the set-man, the point leader, but he was not alone. He had a leadership team that all functioned at varying levels and capacities. We may think that Moses was the pastor, but in fact, he was the apostle. The captains of thousands, hundreds, fifties, and tens were the pastors.

In Deuteronomy 1:9-18, Moses rehearses the episode, but gives us some insight for the need for shared leadership. He confessed "…I am not able to bear you myself alone: how can I myself alone bear your cumbrances, and your burden and your strife". Let's return to Numbers 27. Was Joshua a one-man pastoral leader? No! When Joshua was set before the priest and people, the honour that was on Moses transferred to Joshua. He too must lead and be the point leader with other leaders.

Let's look at this from the New Testament point of view. Among many other scriptures, Acts 15 gives a clear picture that shared leadership was he model in the early church, with a set-man at the helm. When the church was in the earliest stages, there was a debate about the practice of Gentiles keeping the law after conversion. This question created great dissension and dispute and the matter had to be resolved at the council meeting in Jerusalem. Now look carefully at the text: in verse 2 Paul and Barnabas are told to go to Jerusalem to meet the "apostles and elders" to have the matter addressed. Paul and Barnabas arrive and are received by the "apostles and elders". In verse 6 the record shows that the debate rages on while the "apostles and elders" assemble to consider the matter in conference. After testimonies and presentations, James begins to speak in verse 13. By verse 19 he states, "wherefore *my* sentence is …." [emphasis on *my*]. James' words were the final words on the matter. He was the set man, the point leader of the Jerusalem church. Then Luke records that the "apostles and elders" with the church consented with the decision. In verses 24 – 29, the content of the letter sent to the Gentiles uses the plural pronouns "we" and "us", even though James gave the sentence on the matter.

In Titus 1:5, Paul admonishes Titus to set things in order in the churches, he was to ordain elders in every city he went. Remember, the churches in the cities were not single building churches and the elders presided over the various locations of house churches. It was a shared leadership model.

In Acts 20:17-38, Paul sends for the elders at Ephesus. Upon their arrival he admonishes and encourages them to "feed the flock of God" which the Holy Spirit had made them overseers. Here we see a plurality of elders summoned for the task of feeding and overseeing the flock, but in Revelation 2, we read "to the angel of the church in Ephesus". How do we reconcile these two references? The only conclusion to draw is a plurality or shared leadership, with a set man as the first among equals. The elders must feed and oversee the flock.

I have shown you that, in both the Old Testament and New Testament, the composition of leadership was shared. This is the principle for leadership in the Kingdom of God. In both Testaments, the main responsibility of leadership is the care of the people of God through the teaching of the word. A close study of the New Testament clearly shows that no church in the first century was governed by a "one-man" ministry or single "pastor" but, instead, by apostles in conjunction with a shared leadership team of elders. Each local church had scripturally qualified elders, qualified by character, gifts, and "feeding" ability. The spirit worked among them to flow together for recognition and mutual submission. They were able to recognize those who had the ability to teach and speak, in addition to those who could administrate both in temporal and spiritual things. Unity was a key principle by which the church operated. The Holy Spirit governed their attitudes, motives and intentions and then released those for work within their capacity. This is clear in the actions of the leaders in the Antioch church in Acts 13. Luke records there were five leaders who shared the care of the church. They were *prophets* and *teachers* (note two of the five fold ministry offices and the pastor is not mentioned). Together they ministered to the Lord, fasting and seeking the will of God for the assembly. Upon this collaboration in the Spirit, they are directed by the Lord to release Paul and Barnabas for the work God called them to. Verse three details their collective flow and operation... They fasted, prayed, and laid hands on them (laying on of hands was an important part of Apostolic ministry, confirming by all that God had called the workers and that the church was unified in agreement in commissioning them). What we do today in our churches and what the first century apostles did is often light years apart. Some may say this was a natural, historical development of a maturing church. To some degree that may be a valid assessment. However, as stated earlier, the very premise of the actions we practice come from a warped understanding of our primary leadership function. We do not debate maturity, but we challenge the spirit behind that development. When I was growing up, people who acted bigger than their age, and were inappropriate, were called "forced ripe". The idea was that fruits that bare too early were not good for consumption. People who seemingly "matured" early were distasteful to social interactions. The church today still suffers from this malady.

Let's be very honest and realistic about the church's ability to adapt this biblical practice, after so many years of dysfunction and misapplication within our structures and practices. I will be bold enough to share with you the reasons I believe caused this disconnection. However, I encourage anyone, who desires biblical functioning within his or her ministry, to challenge every assumption and man-made obstacle that hinders true revival. I am well aware that the greatest challenge to change in this area of ministry is human nature. A spirit of unity does not naturally govern how we operate, the one-man pastoral system feeds the need in human nature to control and power broker, (meaning the need and use of power to dominate or rule).

It can never be a simple undertaking for a system fed with the power politics of a single leader model, to transition into an equal or shared leadership model. The leaders must be willing to relinquish much of their influence and help create an entirely new culture within the church organization. Any attempt in this direction, requires much prayer and teaching (re-educating) to precede any physical, organizational implementation. Those involved must possess the right spirit, mind and desire for the church of God. I learned this the hard way, from one of our failed attempts at expanding our church into another area. We had spent a little over a year in fasting and prayer as we planned this expansion. The plan was that key young men and their families would be responsible for various elements of the new extension plant. I would remain the set leader, but we would share the responsibility of caring for the saints in the week through small group ministries. We launched, and lasted about one year. Now why did this expansion fail? Time would not permit me here, but the greatest culprit was our failure to teach the model of shared leadership with the same intensity and time we exercised praying for the open door. I later realized that most of the saints that were a part of the launch team still had a one-man pastoral mindset. What we were doing from a vision standpoint was great, but from an implementation standpoint it would inevitably failed. Our team could not function with the shared leadership model, where individuals with particular responsibilities and gifts would minister in their areas of gifting. My responsibility, for teaching and preaching, would be shared as well and we would focus on reaching lost people in the area. However, it imploded. Hindsight is always 20/20. Our team wasn't ready to share leadership; especially not when a few of the men were hoping to be or wanted to be the lead pastor. Two of the young men have since left our ministry and started their own churches, both a one-man pastoral structural system of course.

Absence of Five Fold Ministry

Another element that makes it difficult for this transition to take place is unbelief and fear; these hinder the recognition and acceptance of a true biblical practice beyond the one-man pastoral system. Many people in church circles are afraid of the use of apostolic and prophetic offices and gifting in the church. Many might accept that these offices exist, but may not necessarily believe it is a reality for every church or group of churches. To add to the fear, are experiences of self-styled and appointed apostles and prophets who have run amok with the doctrine of Christ and the people of

God over the last few decades. Let's be transparent. The first century apostles also had to deal with false apostles and prophets, evangelists, pastors and teachers. This never stopped the early church from recognizing these offices and the individuals that occupied them. Secondly, we have more than our fair share of delinquent, self-appointed, divisive, and arrogant pastors; but this has not stopped us from recognizing the office of the pastor. Does that make any sense? Let's face it - the real issue is a serious veering away from the fundamental practice of the apostles of Jesus Christ. The monarchial bishopric, manifested in the power of the office of the pastor, has completely redefined our understanding of apostolic church leadership and most of us can't return, no matter how we confess to the contrary.

Let me make some summative comments about how the combination, of the set-man and shared leadership process, could ultimately and greatly stimulate a strong missional and incarnational reality. The first and foremost responsibility of those called to serve in a leadership capacity, is a total and complete heart for the King and His people. We are called to serve and to be the least among the saints. Secondly, the ministry of the set-man never suggests that he rules by himself. He is the first among equals - a point man with certain skills and gifting, recognized and honoured by other leaders. He possesses a great capacity of personal humility and spiritual integrity, coupled with the professional will to know and execute his primary objective vested in his calling. He is able to temper his heart and authority – never possessing a spirit of an over-lord. In unison, he combines his/her strengths with that of other members of the team. From my research of the Old and New Testaments, it seems that the main responsibility of the set-men was to teach the people the word of God and instruct them in godly living, in addition to spending time with the Lord in devotion and consecration. The set-man should be responsible for vision casting and leading the people in the direction, God has for His people. I believe the clearest New Testament example we have for this is seen in the election of the seven deacons in Acts 6. The dispute arose about discrimination over the food distribution between the Greeks and Hebrew widows. They brought the issue to the apostle to solve. Note the response of the twelve apostles to the church; "...it wouldn't be right for us to abandon our responsibilities for preaching and teaching the word of God to help with the care of the poor..." [Acts 6:1-4 The Message]. The apostles understood their role, they did not allow anything or anyone to distract them from their responsibilities. They remain focused. To burden them with the administrative responsibilities of the church would be spiritual suicide, not just for the apostles but also for the body of Christ, the people.

Allow me to address pastors that may have a gifting outside of the pastorate. Take time to flow into your God given calling. Begin to nurture the gifts in the body, so that those whom God has called around you can begin to support the ministry in ways that will encourage genuine revival. If you are a gifted pastor, recognize that God can and will send those with a particular gifting in the area of apostleship and the prophetic into the house you serve. Release them to function in their God given arena and your ministry will flourish.[56] From this, we will see more church plants, and a missional spirit will drive the church.

Titular Authority

I close this section with a look at a challenging topic, one that threatens to disrupt the genuine spirit of church ministry; the use of titles and names in referring to church leaders. I want to be clear that I am not suggesting in any way that names and titles are not important. The problem is what has occurred over the years because of the misapplication of names and titles, as well as the lack of personal and spiritual integrity, and humility of those with titles.

Let's deal first with the erroneous misapplication of titles and what they have done to the church. Titular authority, at the root, is the power derived from the possession of a title. Conferring a title on someone who may not possess the biblical authority of that title, or who does not have the spiritual gift that accompanies that title, has created many problems in the church. Even more disastrous are the hearts of the men and women who, once infected by this pathos, get hurt and/or hurt others.

---

[56] Please be mindful that I am well aware that there are those who have come into the work of God with ulterior motives and intentions. Those in leadership must be discerning and diligent to prove all things and if following the biblical model for Apostolic leadership is in place then the much feared situations will never be a challenge. The system of the church will eject them out of the system.

As I mentioned before, much of our practices in the church come from non-biblical sources. False religious systems have influenced the church of God and I believe they have violated the word of God, rendering the church powerless on many levels. In Matthew 23:6-10, Jesus commanded his disciples to "...call no man your father on earth; for one is your father, which is in heaven." Yet some religious systems call their priest "Father". In the Protestant world, the title "Reverend" is a popular designation. Are we commissioned or commanded to call anyone Reverend in scripture? The use of titles as legitimate as they are in the kingdom of God, have left the church wounded on many sides. Many seem to believe if a title is vested on them, they are now more significant people or better than others. In many ways, churches encourage that kind of belief system by handing out titles and offices to people who are not called to those offices. In some groups, titles seem to be recognition for years of service.

Much of what I have said up to this point reveals we have misapplied the title "pastor" to much of our work. Take special note: I said misapplied. As previously stated, it is interesting that you will not find any one person in scripture called "pastor". Now this doesn't mean there are no pastors in the church, I would not be so foolish to even suggest that. It is one of the five-fold ascension leadership or headship gifts and offices. Christendom, however, has taken that one office and completely built a religious system around it.

Recently I spoke with a young minister, who is leading a new congregation, about church governance. He stated that he believed local churches should be sovereign and governing their own affairs, which is something I support. However, his response to my question about accountability stood out: "the church is run by the pastor, he hears from God". He was implying that he was solely responsible for hearing from God; is this biblical? Does God speak to anyone else but the pastor? In Acts 13, Luke recorded that "there were in the church in Antioch certain prophets and teachers...as they ministered to the Lord, and fasted the Holy Ghost said..." (1, 2) From here, the Holy Spirit gives instructions for further expansion of the church. No mention of a pastor. The prophets and teachers fulfill the pastoral function. Therefore, it is a bit challenging when pastors seem to believe that God speaks only to them concerning His church. This is not a biblical concept.

Titular power belongs to the spirit of the world, Conner writes. It is a foreign concept to the Bible. We are not called to love the praise of men, which is an attitude titular power seems to promote. I know there are bodies that really discourage the use of titles to avoid this problem, but it seems that somehow the "pastor" title escapes this. The solution to the misapplication of titular authority is to, first, be careful when conferring titles on people. What is more important than the title is the function the title supports. Paul doesn't open his letters with "Apostle Paul..." instead he writes, "Paul, an apostle of Jesus Christ". It is critical to see that the title follows the name. It does not precede it. Why? The title should describe the type of work the individual is involved in, nothing more. Use titles, but be very careful. In many quarters, titles seem to validate some divine endorsement that God is with someone, but very little work is being done. Titles are reduced to status symbols. Ensure that the person, on whom the title is being conferred, has been functioning in some way in the area of ministry connected to the title. What this implies is that the Spirit of God is moving on the individual's life, and is releasing certain qualities in conjunction to the title. For example, a young man in your ministry begins showing a desire for people outside of the local church and God has impressed on him the need of people who live on the street. He begins sharing and befriending the homeless. He seeks no title or publicity in the church. As he serves, the desire and the call become stronger in his heart. He is given direction from God what to do. After some time, possibly years, he realizes that he can serve more in another part of the country or world. He takes courses, improves himself, mentors others, has won some to Christ and has taken some trips and worked in the global field each summer for the past several years. He has demonstrated tremendous leadership and is a model to many. Herein lays a missionary. To lay hands on someone in this situation is the appropriate thing to do. It is not the title that makes him; he has legitimized the authority of that title by obedience to Christ's calling on his life and through steady spiritual growth and maturity.

Characteristics of Leadership

True leadership is different from what we see in many aspects of our culture, and even our churches. Even in the secular world, you have vast differences between good leadership and bad leadership. In Jim Collins groundbreaking study and research *"Good to Great"*, he dedicates an entire section of the study to leadership found in great companies. I was pleasantly surprised to find that leaders in many of the greatest companies exemplified an enormous capacity for personal humility and self-abnegation, amid a strong personal will to do what was necessary for the success of their enterprise. This is the kind of leadership that is modeled in the biblical record. One of the stories that stood out to me was the lifestyle practices of HP co-founders, David Packard and William (Bill) Hewlett. Mr. Packard was a billionaire, but lived in the same house for over 30 years. Bill Hewlett was equally self-effacing, "he drove himself to work and occupied the same office, seemingly with the same furniture for more than forty years,...He was indifferent to the trappings of wealth, but used his to help others and to make good things happen. His wants were remarkably simple and did not seem to be in any way the object of his professional life."[57] These men understood what service really meant and never shied away from building wealth, but understood that wealth was not what made them who they were.

How can an incarnational process work?

An Apostolic – Incarnational - Missional (AIM) Framework

What is an AIM framework? An AIM framework is simply looking at the work of the ministry through the lens of these three theological concepts: APOSTOLIC – INCARNATIONAL – MISSIONAL. Each of these concepts represent and embody a true kingdom building philosophy.

As I have noted, I am staying away from prescribing any specific programs in proposing this AIM framework. It is not a syllabus or curriculum to follow per se; instead, it is a thought process, a way to approach any new idea in any ministerial composition. It can be difficult to use this framework if at the core the ministry/church is not totally committed to the expansion of the Kingdom. Ministries in maintenance mode will be extremely challenged

---

[57] Hewlett.org The William and Flora Hewlett Foundations, by David Pierpont Gardner, 2003

with implementing this framework in their plans. This AIM framework also does not work or make sense if the ministry is not prepared to inculcate its principles at every level of its operations.

This AIM framework, as the term framework suggests, evaluates, and determines all critical actions of a ministry by asking some fundamental questions. Are we staying true to the original intent of Jesus Christ? Are we making ourselves relevant to those in whom we desire to reach, without losing the essence of the faith? Finally, are we committed to going about the work with zeal and fervor in a consistent manner?

Let's look into these separately. The first element of the framework in a ministry is *Apostolic*. Apostolicity encompasses two important aspects, *doctrine,* and *function*. In terms of the doctrine, we do not advocate a philosophy of ministry without a deep-rooted understanding of the primary component of "the message" of the ministry. It is not only what we do and how we do it that matters but also, what we "say" and what we "believe". An Apostolic ministry is a ministry that is rooted in the *theology of the Apostles*. This book does not deal with an orthodox theological explanation of the fundamental doctrines of the church; an excellent online resource can be found at the Institute for Biblical studies.[58] Here the author and other contributors expand on a variety of theological topics.

The other aspect is that of *function*. This is something I will deal with later in more depth, but to be Apostolic literally means, "to be sent". This aspect of the framework is that the ministry must understand its mandate to go into the world with the message of the Gospel. This is a New Testament imperative. The term "world", means *every* part of the world: our communities, regions, and nations. The work of the church is to penetrate the darkness of this world with the glorious message of Jesus Christ. This Apostolic thrust is the product of a daring, risk-taking, church filled with passion and a heartfelt burden and commitment to reaching the lost. The complexity of this is determining how ministries can inculcate the spirit of apostolicity into the daily operations of the church. In other words, is the spirit and the activities in the church fused with the attitude of the church accepting its commission to "go into all the world"; are the actions

---

[58] www.onenesspentecostal.com

that stir the movement of the church based on a corporate mindset to reach outward to the world? This may sound far simpler than it actually is.

The next component of the framework is *incarnationalism*. We studied this concept earlier in this chapter. The application of incarnationalism is fundamentally found in the churches ability to act courageously and valiantly to live out its calling. When a church acts in these ways, not as a mechanical process but more as an organic metabolic process, she will receive the power necessary to be who she is destined to be. Let me explain, we don't have enough ministries in the church to facilitate the amount of ministry needed in the world. We must release people to work incarnationally where God has placed them. The church must possess a genetic stream for sending workers into the field, the place where people live. While doing that, she must embody the spirit of our Lord, transcending the attitude of attactionalism and moving in the power of God into a lost world[59].

---

[59] Plainly stated, incarnationalism is the churches ability to encourage believers to engage with people in the environments in which they live, work and play. For instance, on any given Sunday, parks are filled with families who do not attend church; clubs gather for special interest activities, sporting events etc. An attractional approach to ministry would require those people to leave those events to gather at church. An incarnational approach seeks to reach those people in their own settings. This means the church may need to deputize individuals who are inclined to daring activities to reach the lost. I attended and officiated at a Bikers funeral some time ago, and that experience left a deep impression on me. I walked away from that experience wondering how we would engage a biker sub-culture without stripping them of the passion and love they have for the open road and those monster machines. Fundamentally, there is nothing inherently evil about riding bikes. Jesus came to die for the biker as well. The rigid attitude we have about church attendance has caused us to lose the main message of the Kingdom of God. He came to seek and save the lost. Our attractional approach, has allowed us to support the idea of "us against them"; and although we are fundamentally a "called out" people, our main function remains – to wash ourselves into the fabric of the culture, bringing Jesus Christ with us and to the world; once saved we are no longer of this world, but we remain in it. Jesus taught that the Kingdom of God was like leaven (yeast), which a women (the church) took and hid in three measures of dough until the whole things was filled with leaven Matt. 13:33. Need, we say more? The church is to wash itself so completely into the fabric of the culture until it has completely affected it.

The final aspect of the framework is **Missionalism.** The missional component to the framework is the spirit exhibited by Jesus himself, sent with the task of redemption, infused with ability to heal and to set at liberty those in captivity. The church must be on mission and busy with the task of doing what the Master commands. This is important because not all churches have the same mission. We may share the same general mission, but *how* that mission is carried out differs from assembly to assembly. This is why it is difficult for me to prescribe any specific program. I don't believe in cookie-cutter ministries. The church must find its unique place and service to the world. Therefore, this AIM framework provides the essential components, that if applied properly, offers an enormous imputation of what I call spiritual DNA. This spiritual database contains all the essential information on how the church must act to be a legitimate part of the body of Christ. The divergence of the DNA formulation can be seen in any family unit where there are multiple siblings; father and mother will produce several children and each child carries different formulations of DNA. Therefore, each child is different in size, hair colour, eye colour, and sometimes in skin complexion. Although each child has different features and traits, they are offspring from the same source. This is how the church functions. Although we are all offspring from the same source, we do not all operate in the same way or carry out the same exact mission. The antithesis to mission, is maintenance. Missions is embedded with the genetic seed of "going", "moving", "assignment", whereas, maintenance possesses an inherent need to protect and secure what exists. In essence, maintenance is a retreat mechanism. Missionalism, on the other hand thrives on the adage, "the best defense, is a strong offence".

Incarnationalism and Purpose Driven Churches

Several years ago when I read Rick Warren's book, *Purpose Driven Church,* he talked about the reality that all churches are organized around a particular aspect of the Christian experience. I think he built his case really well for a more attractive model, *Purpose Driven.* Challenged by the work, I made some significant changes to our ministry structure at the time. He proposed that the church should be structured around the major elements of the Christian experience, namely, Outreach and Evangelism, Worship, Fellowship, Congregational development, Discipleship, Christian Education, and Service/Ministry, and each of these elements engages our world. Evangelism engages *the community*; Worship engages *the crowd*, those who attend church gatherings; Fellowship engages the *congregation*; Discipleship engages *the committed*, those who feel an above average call to participate in ministry work on a volunteer basis and Service/Ministry engages *the core*, those called for, and into, direct ministerial work as church staff. Warren was masterful in helping his church, and many others, engage the culture to which they had to do ministry. However, many churches made the mistake of believing in the cookie-cutter approach to ministry. Thousands of churches of all denominational persuasions began copying the Saddleback Church model. What many of them didn't realize was that the Saddleback Church was ministering within a specific cultural setting and using a particular philosophical approach to ministry; one that later we found suspect at best. While we can extract some principles, what churches need to do is discern the will of God and seek for processes that will allow them to engage the culture where they served. Every church must be intimately sensitive to the specific call of God for them and attempt to live out that purpose in ways to reach lives. A successful church in Jamaica, Pentecostal Tabernacle, captures this concept in their mission statement. *"Bring them in, raise them up and send them out!"* This church is keenly aware of its missional responsibility in reaching out to the lost, disciplining those reached and commissioning them for service. It should be noted that, this church is deeply committed to incarnationalism; by working in the community, among the people, and establishing daughter works in many of these communities.

Missional-incarnationalism challenges growth by attraction. The comfort of having large numbers of people attending your church building each Sunday, as an initial strategy for growth, is "at risk". As a church begins to envelope itself in the process of reaching people on their own territory, the gathering of new people in the services becomes less of a desire and ground for success. The gestation period of people who have come in contact with saints could take weeks, even months, meaning some people may not physically come to church for some time. This does not mean people are not being transformed, it just means There is also the risk of investing in projects that may not have an immediate return; putting money into a new project is always a challenging venture. Rocking the boat of pew members, who are accustomed and comfortable with church attendance, while possessing little or no personal commitment for service, is also "at risk". A missional-incarnational model endeavors to put back the primitive spirit and attitude into church practice and thinking. The entire focus of the church should be directed to the distinct mission of Jesus Christ, avoiding an overarching compulsion to attractionalism. The attractional approach of *"Come and see"* is a definite element of church practice. However, in no way should the church center its philosophy and practice of ministry on it. The "come and see" element of church is for fellowship, discipleship, and corporate worship (1 Corinthians 14). Each of these carries a mystical blend of unity and edification of the believers, and exaltation of the Master. By itself though, it leaves a great gap in the church doing her work in the transformation of lives. It is the incarnational approach of the *"go and tell"* element of the church, which gives it its transformational power to a lost world. Let's look at an example.

CHAPTER 7

An Empty Vessel

In the book of 2 Kings chapter 4, there is a story of a widow whose husband died and left her with debts. In order to have the debts settled, the lender was going to yoke her two sons until the debts were paid. This was well within their rights according to Levitical law. The woman appeals to the prophet Elisha, as her deceased husband was himself a prophet. In an effort to engage her in the miraculous ability of God, Elisha asked the women what she had in her possession. She replied, just a little oil. He then commanded the widow to go and borrow as many vessels as she could from her neighbors. She was specifically commanded to borrow as many vessels as she could. When the woman finished collecting the vessels, the man of God commanded her to pour the little oil that she had in the borrowed vessels. As she began to pour, she realized that the oil multiplied and would not stop. The only time the oil ceased was when there were no more vessels left. Elisha commanded the woman to go and sell the oil which had just been supplied, pay off the debts (which included returning the borrowed vessels), and live off the remainder of the profits from the oil sales. *Live off the interest!* This is the language used today within the investment industry. The average person doesn't think that God has that kind of plan for their lives. This was indeed a miracle. God can multiply the oil in times of great need, but without faith and action, God will not work. There are many ways that this story can provide lessons in the ability of God, but permit me to use it as an example that Apostolic churches can use for expanding the kingdom of God.

Imagine the vessels as church systems, the way in which assemblies of people function in replicating the gospel enterprize, church practices. The widow, a type of church, has one vessel with oil in it. The oil is a type of the Holy Spirit. As long as the vessel remains by itself, right side up, there will be a limited supply of oil. It is on the behest of the prophet to go out and seek for other vessels, that the process of multiplication would take place. One important element to Apostolic ministry is a prophetic Word, (there must be a prophetic word over the house of God). God wants to speak to empty vessels! He wants things turned upside down. The widow woman acts on the Word of God by sending her sons to collect as many vessels as they can find. After bringing them back to her home, the word is to take the little oil she possesses and empty it into the other vessels. Miraculously, the oil does not cease, there is an outpouring of the oil, a limitless supply. Each vessel that the woman collected is filled with oil.

This woman could have done something different and she could have looked for ways to maintain the little oil she had. But no, she takes the risk to pour it out! Churches don't see miracles by trying to maintain what little they have, churches will only see miracles when they put everything on the line and pour themselves out. Most churches are paralyzed by fear, and will not go out and plant a new church. Many are afraid to send out young couples to pioneer a new work; afraid to dream impossible dreams; afraid to obey a prophetic word. Some are far too comfortable staying within the confines of sensibility, reasonableness, and safety. Large churches are afraid of losing people, small churches are afraid they will fail and not recover. Wealthy churches don't want to risk losing money on a new project, while leaner churches don't want to be seen as over ambitious and irresponsible.

Many Apostolic churches are no longer willing to take the kind of risk that the widow was willing to take. Maybe desperation can be the mother of the miraculous! There is a measure of faith that comes out of desperate situations. When we realize that there is more to lose than to gain by maintaining the status quo and playing it safe, then the church may act differently. This woman had to act because the lives of her sons were in jeopardy. "If I don't do something, my boys will be sold into slavery". That was enough to kick her into action, to trust the ridiculous instructions of the man of God. It was better than sitting at home fretting about how to keep the boys out of jail. Asking herself, "how could he ask me to go into more debt, to borrow more vessels, knowing I already owe people?" There are no easy answers to those who walk in faith. Your path will be riddled with times of uncertainty, and self-doubt, but, as Donald Trump once said, "you must press ahead, in spite of your personal feelings about your ability".

What does this story teach us about building the church? Among other things, it teaches that, in order to be useful, you must empty yourself. The woman had to empty herself of any personal pride, shame, egoism and humble herself. Until she turned the vessel upside down, the oil stayed as a limited supply. Turning it upside down, allowed God to supernaturally increase its supply. When churches respond to God in faith and are willing to turn themselves upside down, we will see the manifestation of God in His people, turning the world upside down.

Let me propose a potential model for churches that want to grow within their local context, while at the same time remain missional and plant churches. Think of a vessel, in this instant a church, in the midst of many other churches. As this middle vessel fills, it begins to overflow and flows into the other vessels around it. The middle vessel reaches its maximum capacity, but the content never gets stale and stagnant, there is a new and constant flow of the anointing, the spirit, and people. The church is being emptied, but not in the sense that the vessel has become dry and useless. The fluid is being emptied into other vessels who themselves will reach their maximum capacity and need to flow into others. We see this middle vessel as a sending Great Commission church that has divinely understood its sociological limitations; you don't have to be a church with 1000 people before you can be obedient to the Great Commission. Understanding how to turn limitations into opportunities by feeding others, is the genius in multiplying churches. Some of the other vessels will be small, some medium sized and others large. Some of the vessels can even be larger than the middle vessel. However, this will not hinder anyone from becoming a great resource to others. No one should feel intimidated. Everyone can realize growth to the size of his or her vision and dreams.

Years ago, when I was coming up in the ministry, I heard a limiting thought by a Bishop that hindered and perplexed me for years. I can't remember the full context of the discussion, but I know it didn't sit well with me: "...a man never grows any bigger than his father." This "bigger" could mean in influence or the size of a church. To give him the benefit of the doubt, I would say that he was referring to influence, that no matter how great a man becomes, he is still the son of his father. The father is greater because he has given birth to a great son. On the other hand, what if he made the statement, referring to the son's ministry never outgrowing that of his father's? I was not in the pastoral ministry and had no intention of it at the time, but that comment disturbed me. Years later, I thought about how this compared to Joseph's story. After many years of slavery, Joseph finally enjoyed a nobler role than his father in Pharaoh's courts. Then, of course, there was Jesus who said, "greater works then these shall ye do…" referring to the disciples doing more than he in his earthly ministry. The disciples would go further, see more, and experience more than Jesus experienced.

One of the most crippling vices in the church, are fathers who are insecure regarding their sons and use this to hinder any forward progress of the church. God allowed Joseph to dream a much larger dream than Jacob his father. God had a plan for Joseph, and no matter how great a patriarch his father was, the work committed to Joseph's care was something that Jacob could not do. Moses' natural impact is far greater than that of his biological father, Pharaoh and Jethro, men who all played significant roles in his life and had tremendous influence themselves. David outgrew his natural father in both influence and capacity of leadership. Solomon, although not greater in influence than David, expanded the Kingdom beyond that of David; Solomon reigned over a larger territory than his father. This may not be fair, as Jesus was the Messiah, but Jesus outgrew his earthly father's influence. When Jesus died on the cross, there were only two people in his presence, John, the beloved and Jesus' mother, Mary; everyone else had fled. However, on the day of Pentecost, when Peter preached the first message post resurrection, over 3000 people were saved and baptized in Jesus' name. Jesus never had that kind of earthly ministerial success.

In the secular arena, most movie stars are greater than their parents are and many professional athletes reach levels their parents only dreamed. Visit little league baseball diamonds or hockey rinks, and look at every father. They clamor over their sons, and sometimes daughters, to achieve more, run faster, play harder, all in the hope that their child will excel. It's not that every dad or mom out there is a fanatic for their children's athletic future, but I am sure you have heard the stories of parents yelling and fighting at their kids games. I can assure you, it is not just surface excitement; it is a deep longing in a parent, often because they have not lived their own heart's desire. The reality is there are more children that outshine their parents than there are parents who outshine their children. What my dear ministerial colleague was likely inferring is, rarely can a son do the works of a father, but his insinuation was faulty. If the Lord gives the son a greater vision, then the role of the father is to nurture it and allow it to grow to its greatest levels and heights, not be threatened by his own son's ability and capacity. (See how David prepared for Solomon's succession - 1 Chronicles 22)

The tragedy for many churches is, that while the "oil" (the spirit) is flowing over, it begins to empty onto the floor and is wasted because these churches have made no provision for expansion. After a period, the fluid begins to dry up. God will not send fresh oil into a vessel that, once it has reached its capacity, is blind and ignorant to the need of emptying into others. Remember our discussion in chapter 2? Churches that don't reproduce have barren wombs. Eventually, these churches become like the Shunammite women of 2 Kings 4 who, after being barren for years, gives up hope and lives with no expectation at all. Churches that do not have expectation for growth and expansion are churches that will begin to plateau and decline. I have seen firsthand what happens to churches that transition from a strong missional spirit to a maintenance mode. Things begin to dry up. The most desperate attempt in these churches is to find ways of recycling old methods and strategies; attempting to do the old things better, which hardly is the answer.

If we are going to follow the life cycle of any organic life system, there has to be a desire, a compulsion, even an instinct to reproduce. My daughters, although still young are already talking about how many children they would like to have. Churches need to know their stage of life and have a strategy to give birth. I will never devalue the importance of having church buildings, but, unfortunately for many ministries, this is the definition of growth; they bought a building, they built a building, they purchased land, all very notable things, but these should only be a response to the reality of souls being added to the kingdom. Yes, sometimes it is necessary to build the facilities before the people arrive, if that is the assignment over your ministry. However, we should never fool ourselves believing that because we have a building we are a reproducing womb. The Shunammite women mentioned earlier, added a room to her house to accommodate the man of God, but real life came to her with the opening of her womb and giving birth to a son.

Someone may ask the question, "should every church reproduce?" My answer is an unwavering, "Yes!" Every attempt should be made over the lifecycle of a church to reproduce itself. Churches shouldn't even start if they do not have a long term vision of multiplying themselves, and expanding the work of the Kingdom. Churches should start with a mindset to send out workers. My wife and I will spend over 20 years of our lives raising our children, but we are mindful that we are raising them up, to let them go. I am sure their mother and I will struggle to see them go; but, leaving for school, starting their own families, raising their own children are as natural to life as the air we breathe, so we don't question it. Maybe this concept is hard to accept by some because we have been inoculated with the tranquilizing drug of institutionalization and organization, and not organism. Organisms reproduce as a natural process to life; organizations only grow through artificial processes[60].

In closing this chapter, Solomon gives some good advice. Maybe it is more instruction than advice. He writes:

> *"There is that scattereth, and yet increaseth; and there is that withholdeth more than is meet, but it tendeth to poverty. The liberal soul shall be made fat: and he that watereth shall be watered also himself. He that withholdeth corn, the people shall curse him: but blessing shall be upon the head of him that selleth it".* (*Proverbs 11:24-26*)

---

[60] I think it is important for us to stop and think about whose job it is to start new churches. Is it the job of an organization or is it the job of a local assembly? If we say the organization, I think we are going to have some serious challenges. If we say the local church, how is this encouraged? The fellowship I am apart of has wrestled with this. This is mainly because we are still operating in a mechanical mode. The idea of headquarters being involved in the growth of the organization creates many hindrances to growth and movement. When organizations are the only ones responsible for the planting of new churches, it is like grandparents being responsible for having new children or giving birth to grandchildren.

Here are the formulas: scattering equals increase; withholding equals poverty; liberality equals fatness; watering equals being watered; withholding equals curse; giving, even at a price, equals blessing. I found this to be wonderful counsel for ministry development. Churches that withhold when it is time to scatter will experience lack and poverty. Churches that sow seeds will eventually experience increase. The key to prosperity is to understand the principle of times and seasons. In the lifecycle of the church, there will be a time to "plant", a time to "be born", and a time to "cast away stones" (Ess. 3:2, 5). The key is knowing that God has set eternity in the hearts of men. Dr. C.C. Ryrie, the great Bible expositor, said that God has given man the perspective of looking beyond the routines of life and seeing the hand of God at work. When it is time to give birth, we cannot stay the process. God wants children!

SECTION III

Awaken the Sleeping Giant

*Go ye therefore, and teach all nations, baptizing them in
the name of the Father, and of the Son, and of the Holy
Ghost: Teaching them to observe all things whatsoever I have
commanded you: and, lo, I am with you always, even unto
the end of the world. Amen (Matt. 28:19-20)*

*And the angel that talked with me came again, and waked
me, as a man that is wakened out of his sleep. (Zechariah 4:1)*

In this section, I am going to introduce a discussion that will
greatly challenge every reader.. I address this to a specific segment of the
body of Christ, those of you who are intensely committed to the Great
Commission. As you read, think genuinely about how socio-political
and socio-economic constructs have greatly impacted the church's
ability to confront sin and execute the Great Commission. You venture
into the next section, at your own emotional and intellectual risk. On
one level, there are social constructs that need your contemplation
if you sincerely desire to be a kingdom builder. On another level, be
prepared to be challenged, maybe even provoked, to re-evaluate how
you have thought about the Great Commission in the past, in the
context of your religious and church experience. Take into account that
our experiences are not the totality of reality, just "our" reality. Some
may be tempted to dismiss this section as not relevant, as it is not your
issue. This would be a grave mistake; what I address here is something
I believe the entire church must grabble.

Much of what I discuss here, I speak specifically to "***Black churches***".
The challenge I direct to you is to rise above the negative imputations
of social and systemic sin, shake off the subtle but powerful limitations
imposed by your history, (our history) and act in radical obedience to
reach all people irrespective of where you are, or where you are from. Are

we hearing the call of Jesus, *"go into all the world"?*[61] Anglo-Christians, our "white" brothers and sisters in Christ, for centuries have taken up the responsibility of executing the Great Commission to all people. I hope this section will be an impetus for a new wave of mission minded ministries, that will pray and act on the information presented here. It is time to wake up! Don't be trapped or fooled, this is ***not*** a political defense of an ideology, it is a clarion call to impact the world as we know it; although much of what is discussed here is directed to those of African descent, I advise all Christian to read, process and contemplate. This issue is not to be handled in isolation of the extended body of Christ.

---

[61] Allow me to address some of the issues used as an excuse to justify segregation of the church. There are those who will defend this idea by pointing out that Paul was commissioned to the gentiles and Peter to the Jews. Historically and biblically, it is correct; that both these men had callings to different groups of people, but the implication that this supports segregation in the church is quite unfounded. Paul, although commissioned to the gentiles, and as a Jew, was critical in the cross-cultural development of the early church. His theological defense of a unified church is discussed in the letter to the Ephesian. There are those who are bound to think nationalistically, and therefore, are compelled to work among their own people. It is necessary, especial because of language and cultural dynamics. However, this discussion is to broaden the scope of this issue by dismantling some of the sinful elements that hinder the work of ministry, namely, racism, prejudice, and bias.

CHAPTER 8

Wake Up!

The malady of the oppressed: *how oppression
has stifled the mission of the church*[62]

*"Then the eleven disciples went away into Galilee, into a
mountain where Jesus had appointed them: And when they
saw him, they worshipped him: but some doubted. **And Jesus
came and spake unto them**, saying, All power is given unto
me in heaven and in earth. Go ye therefore, and teach **all
nations, baptizing them** in the name of the Father, and of
the Son, and of the Holy Ghost: **Teaching them to observe
all things whatsoever I have commanded you**: and, lo,
I am with you alway, even unto the end of the world.
Amen"** (Matt. 28:16-20)*

---

[62] *Let me warn you, that this chapter is not for the faint at heart. I have considered
removing it from this manuscript but I realized, however, that I would not be true to
my own heart about the matter and my desire to release the hidden power in the church
to fulfill her mandate. By no means is this an exhaustive treatment of the myriad of
issues we face in relation to this subject., I hope to impart some insight,, and someone
will be released to live what they have been feeling regarding the work of the Gospel.
I also note that I do not subscribe to and academic treatment of the label of people
groups. Sometimes, I use the term "black" other times I use the term "African Descent".
I will use the term "white" or "Anglo". There is a need to depart from the categorizing
of people by racial distinctions, it is a serious error in labeling of people.*

One of the, often overlooked, elements of the above scripture is the context in which it was spoken. Jesus has risen from the dead; he is imparting his last assignment for his disciples before ascending into heaven, not to return until the times of the gentiles are fulfilled. He calls the men together and commissions them to the most daunting task imaginable. The task is to establish the Kingdom of God, through the church, here on earth. What I would like us to take some time to observe are some of the critical aspects of the commission not commonly discussed. Specifically, who were these men? Not in terms of their personal identity, family pedigree, careers etc. but more their socio-political and ethnic realities; who was he sending them to? What was Jesus asking these men to do? And, what was going to be Jesus' role in the mission? By answering these questions, we are going to uncover a missing element of the Great Commission that, I believe, has hindered the church's evangelization of the world for the past few centuries. We are then going to close with an analysis of the impact modern sociological vices have had on hindering the church, especially those branches that have identified with, or assumed, an oppression psyche.

I realize that some readers may definitely differ in their views of the issues presented in this section of the book. Without trying to be offensive, some Christians have not had to struggle for liberation the way many others have, so this chapter may challenge them a bit. Sociologically, for example, the concept of "white privilege", (a term not known by many, which we will explore later), has sheltered some Christians from the brutal impact of the chains of oppression. Therefore, they are challenged when trying to understand the deep implications of oppression other Christians unlike them have had to deal with. Talking about this and other issues, and moving from a focus on liberation theology to obeying the Great Commission, ought to be our preoccupation. I am not talking about racial reconciliation; that is an entirely different issue, and I doubt it is

God's plan for the church. We are not called to racial reconciliation[63], we are called to be reconciled to God; Jews and Gentiles alike are together reconciled to God through the finished work of Jesus Christ on the cross. God does destroy the alienation that existed between the Jew and Gentile, and for that matter, any other racial or ethnic conflict, however, the true enmity destroyed was that which existed between God and humanity (Eph. 2:11-19).

With that said, we are going to deal with the Great Commission and who is responsible for its execution. It may seem like I am being political in this section; this is not my chief aim. I do not have a problem with that, but the main point to make here is to explain how four social constructs: colonialism, imperialism, white privilege and liberation theology have worked together to hamper the forward movement of "**the church**". In our carnality, we have successfully fragmented the church into segregated groups resulting in very negative consequences. In the epistle to the Ephesians, the apostle Paul skillfully explains the universal impact of the Cross on the social, psychological, religious, and ethnic barriers to unity. Sin has not only estranged humanity from God, but it has also estranged people from each other. Paul calls the estrangement the "middle wall". Although the "middle wall" Paul discusses in Ephesian was destroyed in

---

[63] Dr. Eric Mason in his blog article "Racial Reconciliation" explains racial reconciliation as "...the restoration of friendly relationships and of peace, where there had previously been hostility and alienation. Ordinarily, it also includes the removal of the offense that caused the disruption of peace and harmony (Rom. 5:10, 2 Cor. 5:19, Eph. 2:16). Although racial reconciliation is not the Gospel or the central focus of it, it is a qualitative application of the Gospel in function and practice". I am going to go a bit further in this discussion. I believe we need more then racial reconciliation. Dr. Mason's definition, which I agree with in part, forces us to ask the question, "When were people groups like 'white and black' ever friendly and now is in need of reconciliation?" Racial Reconciliation is a passive way of dealing with a very tense and deep problem. The church is suspect; it seems to me that the church seeks to continually pacify the real issues for a less conflicting path. We must denounce racial conflict in all its forms and stand behind the cross of Calvary as our unifying code of Arms.

Christ, the church, 2000 years later, still maintains walls of separation[64]. Have modern social constructs demonstrated a greater influence on the execution of the Kingdom priority than what Christ destroyed? Did Christ break down the middle wall of ethnic divide or not? Has the Holy Spirit no power to liberate the church from these destructive chains, or is something else at work? In order to see a true global revival, **the entire church** must awaken from ignorance. There must be a deep and sincere belief that all people groups are in need of salvation, and that all those who have come into that salvation experience are responsible for communicating the Gospel. I envision a church that in its weakness is made strong, that at it's most deprived position, the Holy Spirit will release a surge of apostolic power. Only those who believe, that the middle wall is torn down, will experience this power, and every vice that threatens kingdom advancement will be met with an equal or greater force in the Kingdom of God. Let's begin!

Who were these men?

"And Jesus came and spake unto them…"

A close reading of the Great Commission in Matthew 28 would reveal to us several very important truths. First, the commission was spoken to a group of *oppressed people*. The Romans had oppressed the Israelites for hundreds of years, up to this point. From the time the Greeks were defeated and the Roman Empire flexed its muscles, stretching itself across the then known world, Jewry was under a foreign power. In spite of their political malady, the disciples are ordered by the Master to "go into all the world". Did you hear that? "All the world"; not an insignificant vision. Jesus was passionate about his vision for global impact, a thread that ran from the time of God's promise to Abraham in Genesis 12:1-3, that he would be a father to many nations.

---

[64] The long standing conflict that exist between the Jewish people and the gentiles stood as a representation that sin created alienation between God and men and not until Jesus' death on the cross was the conflict dealt with.

The disciples were not ready for the mission; we could say that at this point they misunderstood the ministry and life of Jesus. It is at the resurrection and the day of the Lord's ascension that we discover the disciples were preoccupied with earthly affairs. They were not considering a spiritual, or an expanded earthly kingdom. They wanted freedom from the oppressive iron feet of the Roman Empire. This oppression drove them behind closed doors in the days subsequent to the crucifixion.

> *"When they therefore were come together, they asked of him, saying,* **Lord, wilt thou at this time restore again the kingdom to Israel?** *And he said unto them, It is not for you to know the times or the seasons, which the Father hath put in his own power. But ye shall receive power, after that the Holy Ghost is come upon you: and ye shall be witnesses unto me both in Jerusalem, and in all Judaea, and in Samaria, and unto the uttermost part of the earth".* (Acts 1:6-8)

Notice their question, "wilt thou...restore...the kingdom to Israel?" They had no thought of mission to lost people; they were consumed with nationalistic interests. They couldn't see beyond their socio-political dilemma, which was steeped in anti-Semitic sentiment. The feeling was so deep that the Zealots believed the only way to overcome Rome was with violence. I could imagine that Simon, the Zealot, was following Jesus with mixed feelings; hearing Jesus teach about peace and love, while in his heart waiting for the day that Jesus would lead the troops to battle against Rome. Remember, the Romans ultimately sentenced Jesus to death by execution. The Jews had no power to enforce capital punishment without Roman approval, hence, they sought Pilate to grant the execution order.

So, we see a very interesting aspect of the Gospel enterprise. God does not call men because they are a part of a dominant group. The calling of God is not based on political influence, economic strength, or ethnic background. People are called to world mission despite their socio-political status.

Who was he sending them to?

"...all nations..."

The commission is given to Jews (not Anglos) in its origin. Here they are commissioned to go beyond their own cultural ethos and structures to worlds unknown; where language, culture, customs and values differed. The force of the commission is so strong, that it seems to negate any inherent cultural, economic and socio-political elements that would render it ineffectual. In other words, Jesus sends them to regions beyond their borders to people who do not speak their language, do not share cultural practices or religious heritage.

In Acts 1:8, the Lord repeats the scope and catchment to which he is sending them, *"...and ye shall be witnesses unto me both in Jerusalem, and in all Judaea, and in Samaria, and unto the uttermost part of the earth."*

Irrespective of social constructs, the commission demands total and impervious allegiance. We cannot say we are poor, uneducated, not a part of some patrician fraternity, and therefore unable to fulfill the Great Commission. The commission supersedes those sentiments. My mind races to the experience of Philip and the Ethiopian in Acts 8. What are we to make of this cross-cultural transmission of the Gospel? It surely flies in the face of those who believe Europeans brought the Gospel to the African continent. Here is the powerful story of a Eunuch under the Queen of Ethiopia, Candice, receiving the apostolic message of the Kingdom of God, the life, death, burial and resurrection of Jesus. He accepts the gospel through Philip's preaching, commanding his chariot be stopped so he could be baptized. He is baptized by Philip and continues into Ethiopia[65]. I have had the honour of sharing fellowship with the inheritors of that great Ethiopian movement that today encompasses well over 3 million

---

[65] It is noteworthy to mention the issue of race relations in the bible is a very different issue than what we must grabble with in the 21st century. In the bible, the issue of conflict between people groups was more directed to religious beliefs and deities than on ethnicity. Very few people are aware that both Moses and Joseph married black African women. There was no racial tension between the Ethiopian Eunuch and Philip, a Jewish apostle. Any racial tension that existed in scripture had its roots in some form of religious beliefs.

saints, If these Jewish disciples were sent to "all nations" by the Lord, what does that teach us about our responsibility? I can only imagine what this world would be like if everyone with a revelation of the commission would shake off the chains of oppression, both physical and mental, and fulfilled its full mandate. Even better, what kind of churches would be born? Let me make this crystal clear. When people groups (as opposed to just a single individual) accept and receive the Gospel message and are empowered by the Holy Spirit to continue to advance the Kingdom,[66] that people group has the same mandate as the early church in fulfilling the Great Commission. This is a critical element to the Gospel enterprise. The thrust of the Spirit in the execution of the commission is to move people with an apostolic drive, a compulsive sending and going; go into the next village, town, district, city or nation with the message of the Gospel. The spirit doesn't sit still, idle and complacent; He compels men and women to "go". "Going" is an action word, requiring movement. So this oppressed group, Jewish men, is sent with an assignment to cultures, peoples, and nations different in every way from their own.

What was Jesus asking these men to do?

"...baptizing them...Teaching them to observe all things whatsoever I have commanded you..."

This aspect of the commission teaches us something really wonderful and revealing. It is not just that people should be baptized in water- it is definitely that, but it speaks of a more enduring element of apostolic ministry: the establishment of congregations. You will recall that, when John the Baptist baptized in the Jordan, the people became his disciples. Why? Because baptism was more than just the act of being immersed in water, it was identification with the baptizer and his teaching. Once the candidate was baptized, they became students of the baptizer. This is what we commonly call discipleship today. Jesus was commanding the

---

[66] When someone is saved there needs to be time for discipleship. This is also a systemic process within people groups; time must be given to that group to mature and for the Holy Spirit to lead them into a missional strategy.

disciples to establish communities of faith and, in those communities, teach the people the doctrines of the faith. It is important to know, in the Hebrew culture, teaching was intrinsically connected to action. These men understood that they were to teach the people how to live, which also involved practicing their faith.

Jesus commanded his disciples to do many things: he taught them how to live with each other and God (the beatitudes); he instructed them to love each other; to heal, raise the dead, baptize, pray, read, fellowship, worship, and to consistently reach lost people.

A very close look at Paul's ministry reveals the establishment of the church throughout Asia. The early church was extremely mission driven, while they lived out the life of the Spirit. It is very important to understand that missions was not, and is not, an add-on to church programs. The church was born and established with a missional spirit and decree. Mission doesn't happen with a special church campaign. It happens when every person who has encountered Jesus reflects him in everyday life. This was how the early church grew rapidly. Yes, there was a missional strategy involving corporate giving, sending, and supporting of workers; these two concepts worked hand in hand to move the work of the Kingdom forward.

What was going to be Jesus' role in the mission?

"...and, lo, I am with you always, even unto the end of the world. Amen".

Two things stand out here, *presence* and *duration*. First, Jesus promises that he was going to be an active *presence* in the work he had committed in their hand. So, in the process of going, baptizing and teaching, Jesus would be working with them. This is exciting, because his promise is weaved into the entire commission. When they were "going", he would be with them. This is not a casual sitting with them on a ship or some donkey ride across the country side, going from one place to another. I believe it speaks of our journeys through adverse situations, in places where we may not be welcome. When we look at Paul's journey, we see his voyages filled with adverse weather conditions, delays, near-death experiences and misunderstandings. Jesus promises to be with them as he promises to be with us, as we establish faith communities. In the process of planting churches, with all its complexities, lack of resources, and shortages of labourers, there is a promise of his presence. There is also the process of teaching those who have received the Gospel message. The Gospel is hid from those who do not seek it; it is the Lord's responsibility to reveal the truth to His people, He opens their understanding so they can understand the scriptures (Luke 24:45).

Then secondly, Jesus speaks of *duration,* he says *"…unto the end of the world*[67]*".* Surely, he knew that this band of disciples were not going to live forever; here is a revelatory truth that we must grasp. When he says that he would be present with them, "even until the end of the world", he speaks of apostolic succession. This is not in the sense of pontification, as in the Roman Catholic church, but in the sense of believers of apostolic teaching continuing to fulfill the commission until the return of Christ, at the end of the age, the *Parousia.* Jesus promises that he will actively work with those who take the task to heart; he will be with us as we fulfill the Great Commission until the end of the age. Apostolic succession is critical in understanding the continuity of the work. We run our leg of the race during this age, but the age will supersede us, others must run what is entrusted to them. This is a powerful realization, and a word that should prick our hearts and move us to action in fulfilling this great Gospel assignment.

To conclude, we see something dynamic happening, something hid, a missing link as it were. First, Jesus calls men from a class of social outcasts, not merely who are individually weak, but from a collectively weak group.

---

[67] There are two Greek New Testament words translated by the single English world "world". The Greek work *kosmos.* A *kosmos* is something, which is in proper order or harmony, something that enjoys proper arrangement. *Kosmos* in the most common Greek usage is the world as the sum and total of everything constituting an orderly universe. The other word is *aion,* from which the English word eon is derived. Aion has no connotation of an order or a structure but designates a period and ought to be translated by the English word "age". (Ladd, 1959) Therefore, Jesus is not dealing with the physical structure of creation, but instead of a period of time. It is very important to understand, that this gives us a very clear picture of the span of time Jesus is going to be with us to the end of the age. We do not have time to deal with this but "this age", the world, or *eon* Jesus is referring to ends at the second coming of Jesus Christ. Therefore, this *duration,* and the promise of his presence stands at this very hour.

They are not sent on this mission with a bag of money and world class resources. Instead, Jesus lays on them the audacious goal of reaching *the World* [68]with the Gospel, and all he gives them is a promise; no thought to linguistic, cultural, religious or economic barriers, just a huge vision and mission for the world. But, he binds the Great Commission with an inspiring promise; one that every one of us who work frontline for God should hold dear to our hearts, *"… lo I am with you always…"* Wow! Yes, those you preach to may not want to accept the Gospel because of your skin colour, social status, or even your gender. Your consolation, however, is that, as long as you are obedient and faithful to the commission, Jesus is with you. What a wonderful promise to those who are engaged in the work of the Lord!

---

[68] Here *kosmos*, the structure of the world system; which includes people.

CHAPTER 9

Awaken the Sleeping Giant!

I want to weave elements of the statements from the previous chapter with an analysis of how modern socio-cultural and political abuses have damaged and hampered the fulfillment of the Great Commission. People affected by colonial and imperialist constructs have a significant contribution to make to the Gospel enterprise, but must first deal with the centuries old impediments locked deep within the subconscious spirit. I will be very blunt, so there is no confusion about what I am trying to communicate. I understand the Great Commission to be an enormous facet to the Gospel enterprise and, therefore, it needs the attention of our keenest faculties spiritually, intellectually and physically. Since the Great Commission is so important, we cannot ignore those responsible for its execution. Here we will deal primarily with those of African descent and their response to the Great Commission, with inferences to other people groups who have a history of oppression, namely, Latin Americans and Native Indians of the Western hemisphere[69]. This analysis will focus particularly on four social constructs: colonialism, imperialism, liberation theology, and white privilege, examining how these vices have affected the fulfillment of the Great Commission by those from African, Caribbean and Latin American cultures.

---

[69] Whenever we deal with oppression there must be a discussion of the oppressor. However, the scope of this book doesn't cover that conversation. Suffice to say that I am dealing with a systemic oppression imposed by the modern slave experience and its impact on a group of people.

Alan Todd

Colonial and Imperial impacts on the Great Commission

In defining colonialism, we look at its root, "colony", which comes from the Latin word *colonus*, meaning "farmer". The practice of colonialism usually involved the transfer of population to a new territory, where the new arrivals lived as permanent settlers while maintaining political allegiance to their country of origin. Imperialism, on the other hand, comes from the Latin term *imperium*, meaning, "to command". Thus, the term imperialism draws attention to the way that one country exercises power over another, whether through settlement, sovereignty, or indirect mechanisms of control.

Both colonialism and imperialism are not modern phenomena; world history is full of examples of one society gradually expanding by incorporating adjacent territory and settling its people on newly conquered territory. The ancient Greeks set up colonies as did the Romans, the Moors, and the Ottomans. This fundamental idea existed even among native peoples and people indigenous to the entire world's continent, albeit, it would not have been characterized the same way. Colonialism and imperialism, then, are not restricted to a specific time or place. Nevertheless, in the sixteenth century, colonialism and imperialism changed dramatically because of technological developments in navigation that allowed those from the "known world" to connect to more remote parts of the globe. Fast sailing ships made it possible to reach distant ports while sustaining ties between the main colonial center and its colonies. The modern European colonial project emerged when it was possible to move large numbers of people across the Atlantic ocean, and maintain political sovereignty in spite of geographical dispersion (i.e. the slave trade enterprise and migration of European citizens). The terms colonialism and imperialism describe the process of European settlement and political control over the rest of the world, including the Americas, Australia, and parts of Africa and Asia.[70]

One of the elements of colonialism and imperialism is the idea of *dominance*. It should be clearly stated that the Great Commission, given by Jesus, is not a commission for any one culture to dominate another. The Great Commission is the transmission of the Gospel of the Kingdom

---

[70] Worldwide web Source, First published Tue May 9, 2006; author unknown

of Jesus Christ into every culture and ethnicity, without stripping that culture of its distinctiveness. This is what we call *contextualization* of the Gospel; communicating the Gospel in ways that neither destroy nor damage the host culture. However, the Gospel does extract elements of culture that is intrinsically tied to sin. This is called *systematic sin;* it is sin that is embedded in ideologies, ways of life, mores and values that are in defiance to God and His natural and moral laws.

This domination element was core to the European slave enterprise; this enterprise was quite different than that practiced in the Roman Empire in the first century. This slavery was marked by very dehumanizing treatment of one people group by another group. The economic implications of the trade perpetuated the system and the church did not emerge in her full identity and strength to resist the movement. Sin wove itself into the very fabric of the slave movement and the church was not able to contend with a more vigorous fight for righteousness.[71] While this book is not written to explore the long, and at times, depressing history of slavery, it must be stated that, in the psyche of the slave, was deep-seated self-hate and feelings of inferiority. Deep down, one of the most destructive forces against a broader application of the Great Commission was this psychological impediment in both the slaves and the masters of that era who confessed Christianity. Even with that conflict, however, many black preachers crossed the colour line, a testament to the power of the Gospel and its liberating affect. Equally significant are the stories of many

---

[71] Those who held the true spirit of God in their hearts made valiant efforts. There are stories of those that against all odds persisted to do the will of God. The stories of black preachers are vast and exciting to say the least. For example, Jarena Lee, born in 1783 in Cape May, New Jersey, as a freeborn child became a powerful and influential black female preacher. "Lee became a black sermonizer, an exhorter who spread the Gospel in places few black women had ventured, sharing her love of God with blacks, **whites,** and native Indians. She travelled north to New England and Canada, took steamboats to Delaware and Maryland. She preached in Buffalo and New York City. She traveled hundreds of miles any direction she could, often on foot. During one year, she traveled more than two thousand miles and delivered 178 sermons" C. Johnson and P. Smith, *Africans in America*, WGBN Educational Foundations, 1998, page 292

white believers who, because of Christ, openly contested the evils of the slave system. The question for us is why we have not progressed further than these early mavericks. This is not a political question. Today the President of the United States of America, Barack Obama is the first African American to hold this office: so surely, the wheels of change are in full swing. I am contending, however, for something deeper, more prolific and nobler than black or female world leaders, I am probing 'into this questions as it relates to the Great Commission. Why is it that, well over 200 years after slavery, churches in North America at 11:00 am are still the most segregated places in the world? There are black presidents, black world leaders, extremely high profile athletes, CEO's of major corporations both male and female, leading black and non-black people; how is it that the church, particularly the "black" and other ethnic minority churches, have failed to step into that noble calling and act in full obedience to the Great Commission? Why are "black and Hispanic churches" not more visible in leading pioneering mission works in non-black, non-hispanic countries, communities and cities? Are we waiting for permission? That has already been given - (Matthew 28:19; Mark 16:15; Luke 24:46-49: John 20:21; Acts 1:8).

The psychological impediment mentioned earlier may be the culprit. It has demobilized and demoralized oppressed groups, hindering them from acting on the words of Jesus. According to Johnson and Smith (1988), "As early as the 1800's Blacks sensed that they would never be considered full-fledged members of society"[72]. Researchers George Barna and Harry Jackson confirm this. In their research, they found that although blacks have achieved socio-political status on par with whites and Hispanics, they felt deeply that they were not accepted in the mainstream of society as far as beliefs, customs and values were concerned. For the Black population, Barna and Jackson found that Blacks felt [73] it was only "...reasonable... that blacks would go where they have the greatest chance of gaining a

---

[72] C. Johnson and P. Smith, *Africans in America*, WGBN Educational Foundations, 1998, page 275

[73] Am I right to assume that to a great extent this dilemma remains a current issue? I believe it is.

hearing for the Gospel."[74] The underpinning point here is that the Black consciousness has been beaten down by psychological rejection, hindering the Great Commission's execution from this part of the church. We will see in the next chapter the fruits that this kind of impact has had on the task of the great commission. As stated, on January 20, 2009, an African-American became the 43rd president of the United States, 90% of churches led by Black leaders remain 100% Black in membership. This is not just a Black dilemma; other people groups must also face these challenges and work to abolish them, including our "white" -counterparts. If we analyze the number of Black churches that are doing missions in non-Black countries, unfortunately very little is being done. However, that shouldn't be a surprise; Barna and Jackson found that "...outside of family members, blacks are most likely to assume an affinity for matters of faith with other blacks. It is almost as if blacks view Christianity as a faith experience that only they can truly comprehend because of what blacks have endured for so many years as a result of slavery, prejudice, and economic disadvantage"[75]. In the past, the solution was to defer their dream. Slaves figured the only way to progress their desire for the Gospel was to join groups that were going somewhere, and would not isolate them from participating in the Great Commission. Black church leaders and believers began stressing the need for a luxurious life of faith without white people.[76] Even today, this belief buried deep in the subconscious of modern Black church leaders, is a current reality. I have heard ministers grapple with this issue with statements to the affect, "why try, they ("white" believers) are in God's hands, they don't have any interest in us" or "we should focus on who is in front of us" The black church's strategy became very internally driven, and

---

[74] Time doesn't permit to expand on the impact of evolutionary theory in bolstering the colonial enterprise. Author Ken Ham, CEO and President of Answers in Genesis has produced some excellent resources to deal with this issue, particularly a video resource entitled: Foundations: One Blood, One Race.
G. Barna and H. Jackson, *High Impact African-American Church*, Regal Books, 2004 pg. 115

[75] ibid

[76] I C. Johnson and P. Smith, *Africans in America*, WGBN Educational Foundations, 1998

in many quarters, remains this way today. In the past, even if there were challenges in language and culture, the binding tie was shared experience as an ethnic group. This has persisted and therefore, most Black churches in the West continues to keep its focus on its own communities; in the Caribbean, church leaders leave the Islands and seek to do ministry almost exclusively to ex-pats; North American Blacks seek missions and ministry opportunities in countries in Africa, where the need for Western support and guidance is high. Doesn't something seem wrong with this picture?[77]

Either directly or indirectly, the Black church has sabotaged its own destiny. They profess a vision for a strong missional strategy, but do not take seriously the mandate of the Great Commission beyond cultural or ethnic similarities. This is unfortunate because in the past several decades there has been such a drastic change in socio-political attitudes, along with economic developments, paving the way for many opportunities for cross-cultural ministry. The time is right for Blacks to extend themselves, and, with deep spiritual heritage, zeal and vigour, thrust themselves into a Kingdom vision for the execution of the Great Commission. Asia, Europe, South and Central America are ripe fields for the dissemination of the apostolic message and, if I may be frank, that job is not restricted to Anglo-Christians. If, in the past, the direct and indirect resistance of white Christians hindered the so-called "black" church, through prejudicial social constructs, we are now long past this. It is now on our

---

[77] I am a strong believer in the ability groups have in reaching out to their own. There are cultural, and linguistics elements that make it possible to reach and communicate with people of similar backgrounds. Even in our North American context, there are opportunities to do ministry among cultural groups that are best served by people from those same groups. This proposition does not rule that out. What I am constantly contending for is something broader, larger, more encompassing than just a simple "we need to help our own" attitude or solution to a very large and complex problem. Jesus at one point told the disciples not to go to the gentiles. They were only to go to the "lost sheep of the house of Israel". The New Testament is an excellent example of the churches ability to scope the division of labour; Peter and others would focus on the gospel to the Jews, while Paul and others to the gentiles. Today, we should be no less inclined. Some ministers are nationalistic, they cannot see beyond their own group. That is fine. We just cannot allow that to bind us to a very limited view of our total mission – the gospel to the *world.*

own cognizance to bear the burden of a world lost without Christ. What Anglo-Christians possessed, which led to their engagement in the great commission, was a faulty belief that colonialism was a privilege of divine calling. This thinking is something we know was not present in the psyche of those of African descent. Africans or other people groups have never had a compulsion to dominate *the world*.

The question that remains to the church, of every people group, is, *"what is the intrinsic power of the Great Commission?"* Is it not the spirit inspired compulsion to spread the message of Jesus Christ to the world? There must be a consciousness in every people group, with whatever resources afforded them, to engage the Great Commission with total world vision and passion.

The next social construct that further hampers the execution of the Great Commission by oppressed groups is the impact of liberation theology.

Liberation Theology

Quite surprisingly, liberation theology was born out of the Roman Catholic tradition. It is a political movement interpreting the teachings of Jesus, in relation to liberation from unjust economic, political, and social conditions. In the 1950-60's, the poverty that affected certain communities in Latin America created a moral outcry in the ranks of Catholic leaders. They felt the need for a way to understand and address the suffering of the poor, beyond religious passivity. Father Gustavo Gutierrez, a Peruvian priest, wrote one of the movement's first responses, *A Theology of Liberation*. In it, he clarifies liberation theology as; "an interpretation of the Christian faith through the poor's suffering, their struggle and hope, and a critique of society and the Catholic faith and Christianity through the eyes of the poor". Oppressed people, who had suffered and struggled to free themselves from the chains of the oppressor, felt compelled to utilize liberation theology as a response to their challenges; they wanted to free themselves from the power of the oppressor, and live in freedom. This was also the cry of the first century disciples following the resurrection of Christ. The consuming thought of those early Apostolics was not mission, as much as it was liberation. "Will you at this time, restore the Kingdom to Israel..." (Acts 1:6) was their query to the resurrected Lord. Rome had choked Israel for centuries and the Zealots and others were ready for freedom. However, Jesus set the record straight, "I didn't come for you to consume yourselves with ideas of liberation...I came that the glorious Gospel would be spread to the ends of the earth, and it is with you, the oppressed, that I will accomplish this task...". "You shall receive power, to be witnesses unto me...in Jerusalem, Judea, Samaria, and the uttermost part of the world" (Acts 1:8). The backdrop to this scripture is the Old Testament understanding of the Lord's pronouncement, *"not by might, nor by power, but by my spirit says the Lord"* (Zech. 4:6). It's not politics, or economic strength that will set people free, it will be the Spirit of the Highest! How is that for liberation theology?

Liberation Theology has developed into something broader than its original definition but its roots provide a suitable understanding of some keys issues. The Master is not concerned with my individual liberation; he is concerned with liberating those bound by the power of sin. Jesus points the early church in the direction of this mission. While preoccupied with self-preservation, Jesus is challenging the church to self-sacrifice. Isn't it interesting that he calls the oppressed to minister to both the oppressor and oppressed?

In a more modern context, we cannot properly understand the plight of the "black church" or any other oppressed group without spending time to uncover this concept as it relates to the struggle to fulfill the Gospel mandate.

What is Black Liberation Theology?

Anthony Bradley, a research fellow at the Acton Institute and assistant professor of Apologetics and Systematic Theology at Covenant Theological Seminary in St. Louis, and probably the foremost authority on the subject, writes that,

> "Black theology is a theology of black liberation. It seeks to
> plumb the black condition in the light of God's revelation
> in Jesus Christ, so that the black community can see that

the Gospel is commensurate with the achievements of black humanity. Black theology is a theology of 'blackness.' It is the affirmation of black humanity that emancipates black people from white racism, thus providing authentic freedom for both white and black people. It affirms the humanity of white people in that it says 'No' to the encroachment of white oppression"[78].

At face value, Liberation Theology seems like a good and noble pursuit. The disciple's interest in nationalistic freedom can hardly be frowned upon; It's only natural that one would seek freedom from an oppressor, however the challenge with Black Liberation Theology is its preoccupation with the spirit of victimization. The pursuit to be free is every man's right. Jesus, however, seems to expect a very different order of priorities for those who have come into relationship with him. We are not suggesting that oppression is to be encouraged and go unchallenged; the Kingdom of God is the Kingdom of righteousness, justice, and peace. The danger is a liberation that is one sided. True liberation must liberate the oppressor as much as the oppressed. Black Liberation Theology seeks to liberate the oppressed but holds the oppressor suspect of any ability to change. Bradley states that "...while Black Liberation Theology is not main stream in most black churches, many pastors in the generation *of the 60's and 70's [and I would say even earlier]* are burdened by the weight to shed themselves from the oppression of the dominant white oppressor". In my earlier years in church, I remember hearing some preachers make statements that resonated with a disdain for white people. These were truly anointed men, but somehow the imprint of victimization left resentment in their hearts. I hasten to add, this is not a one sided issue. It is clear that the impact of ethnic discrimination has done much to harm the church's ability to accomplish the Great Commission.

Bradley further writes that, "Black Liberation Theology actually encourages a victim mentality among blacks." John McWhorters' book *"Losing the Race"*, is helpful here. Victimology, says McWhorter, is the

---

[78] Article: The Marxist Roots of Black Liberation Theology *http://www.acton.org/pub/ commentary/2008/04/02/marxist-roots-black-liberation-theology*

adoption of victimhood as the core of one's identity—it is expressed in one who suffered living in "a country and who lived in a culture controlled by rich white people. It is a subconscious, culturally inherited affirmation that life for blacks in America has been in the past, and will be in the future, a life of being victimized by the oppression of whites. In today's terms, it is the conviction that, 40 years after the Civil Rights Act, conditions for blacks have not substantially changed"[79]. Some would debate that a Black President is an allusion of real and lasting change, while others would say that it is proof we have come a long way in the liberation from the chains of the oppressor. The overall result, says McWhorter, is that "the remnants of discrimination hold an obsessive indignant fascination that allows only passing acknowledgement of any signs of progress." The perpetuation of a cultural identity born out of self-loathing and anxiety is often preoccupied with inventing reasons to cry "racism", rather than working toward changing social mores, and often inhibits any movement toward reconciliation.

Some may say that the oppression the disciples of the first century encountered was mild compared to that of the Africans' slavery and oppression, and with some justification. But, I cannot accept that once people come into the transformative power of the Gospel with all its resident power, they should remain a victim to **any** vice; I refuse to give sin that much power. There must be a deep healing of the spirit and soul, possible only as a result of the transforming work of the Holy Spirit in one's life. This is followed by a coming of age, a maturing into the full stature of the measure of Christ, as Paul states. This is a liberation way beyond ethnic, cultural or economic boundaries. Honestly, grappling with these issues is a must for any and every one interested in freeing all people to live the life God desires for them. From my experience, many in the body of Christ only offer lip service to the prospect of making the changes necessary for true obedience to the Great Commission.

Let's turn now and deal with the final issue in the discussion of impediments to the execution of the Great Commission, the subject of "White Privilege".

---

[79] Article: The Marxist Roots of Black Liberation Theology*http://www.acton.org/pub/commentary/2008/04/02/marxist-roots-black-liberation-theology*

White Privilege

White Privilege as a sociological concept, which describes advantages purportedly enjoyed by white persons beyond what is commonly experienced by non-white people in those same social, political, and economic spaces (nation, community, workplace, income, etc.). It differs from racism or prejudice in that a person benefiting from white privilege does not necessarily hold racist beliefs or prejudices themselves. Often, the person benefiting is unaware of his or her privilege.

In the late 20th century, issues of "whiteness" and its (never before discussed) elements began to emerge. In his 1935 book, *Black Reconstruction in America*, W. E. B. Du Bois first described the "psychological wages" of whiteness:

> It must be remembered that the white group of laborers, while they received a low wage, were compensated in part by a sort of public and psychological wage. They were given public deference and titles of courtesy because they were white. They were admitted freely with all classes of white people to public functions, public parks, and the best schools. The police were drawn from their ranks, and the courts, dependent on their votes, treated them with such leniency as to encourage lawlessness. Their vote selected public officials, and while this had small effect upon the economic situation, it had great effect upon their personal treatment and the deference shown them. White schoolhouses were the best in the community, and conspicuously placed, and they cost anywhere from twice to ten times as much per capita as the colored schools. The newspapers specialized on news that flattered the poor whites and almost utterly ignored the Negro except in crime and ridicule.[80]

---

[80] W. E. B. Du Bois, *Black Reconstruction in America, 1860-1880* (New York: Free Press, 1995 reissue of 1935 original), pp. 700-701..

Today, we look back at those conditions and realize the gross injustice. But the repercussions of those attitudes, in a very subtle way, gave permission to later generations to be completely blinded to how they continue to benefit from these wages. Coupled with this subtle disposition of privilege, was the more overt sense of superiority that the "privilege" of being white brought with it. This stemmed from the roots of "racism", which had always been a part of the body politic and social construct. This also affects the self-esteem. Beverly Daniel Tatum points out that most white people do not think of describing themselves as "white" when listing descriptive terms about themselves, whereas people of colour usually use racial or ethnic identity descriptors. One way we verify this is by examining the many forms we fill out in our culture. When these forms seek information about our demographical make up or racial statistics, rarely is the term 'White' a selection option. However, we will see African American, Black, Asian, Native Indian or other. Tatum suggests this is because the elements of one's identity that are congruent with the dominant culture are so normalized and reflected back at them, that they are apt to take such traits for granted. In reality we will see this sociological behaviour in any culture and country where there is a dominant ethnicity, whether it is African (Black), Asian, or Hispanic.

Tatum writes that dominant micro-cultures, in this case "white" people, set the parameters in which "subordinate" micro-cultures operate. Subordinate groups are often labeled as substandard in significant ways: e.g., Blacks have historically been characterized as less intelligent than Whites. Subordinates are also defined as being innately incapable to perform the preferred roles in society.[81] I don't mean to suggest that little progress has been made. But, the deep seated impact of these social constructs are so cavernous, we cannot escape their far reaching effect on the lives of people and its ensuing challenge to the church.

---

[81] Tatum, Beverly Daniel (1999-06-18). *Why are all the Black Kids Sitting Together in the Cafeteria? And Other Conversations About Race*. New York: Basic Books.

The Persistence of White Privilege

In her personal account of experiencing white privilege, Heidi A. Zetzer, the Director of the Hosford Counseling & Psychological Services Clinic at the University of California, Santa Barbara, explains why white privilege is such a persistent problem. She categorizes it as an "institutional and individual manifestation of racism, however indirect or unintentional."[82] This indirectness of white privilege is what makes it so prevalent. If people are not educated on the matter, it is unlikely that they will take note of it. Secondly, those that are aware of it, suffer under the stigma of benefiting from an unfair system. Zetzer asks, "How can I see myself as a just person when I willingly participate in a system that is inherently unfair?" The guilt experienced by this realization does not motive its, recipients to look for ways to solve the problem. "White guilt," as Zetzer deems it, is actually an impediment to change. Consequently, even if people become educated on white privilege, it is unlikely that they will take action to change, instead they will allow the problem to persist.

Zetzer outlines the changes that are necessary to make progressive steps in dealing with white privilege and its implications. She notes that most people who are educated about white privilege undergo a first-order change; they gain increased awareness, knowledge, and skills. However, progress towards equalizing an unjust system like white privilege, requires individuals to undergo second-order change. Second-order change is characterized by a paradigm shift where people use their awareness, knowledge, and skills to take action. Zetzer believes the first, and easiest, way to initiate this transformation is through dialogue. Honest and multicultural dialogue is the first way to build alliances, which can then

---

[82] Zetzer, H.A. (2005). White Out: Privilege and Its Problems. In S.K. Anderson & V.A. Middleton (eds.), Explorations in Privilege, Oppression, and Diversity (pp. 5). Belmont, CA: Thomson Brooks/Cole.

"transform people and systems and turn intention into action," thus slowing the persistence of white privilege.[83]

What does this have to do with the Great Commission? How does white privilege affect the church's response to being a truly transformative entity? White privilege and the Gospel endeavour seem to carry two fundamental challenges. The more overt attitudes of white privilege is in fact "racial" superiority – contributing to the notion that the expansion of the Gospel endeavour was somehow the responsibility of Anglo-Christians. This coupled with the colonial enterprise, fed an imperial mindset, which deemed other cultures and people groups less than human. The consequences of this notion has been extremely damaging both for White and non-White Christians. White Christians have developed a false sense of superiority, believing that the task of the Great Commission is "their" job. Non-white Christians fail to see beyond the currently held belief: that the task of the Great Commission is theirs to spread only to those "like themselves". The less overt attitudes, almost derisorily, convinces Whites that nothing is wrong. Therefore, most of the dialogue in the Christian

---

[83] This is the key work of the church today. We need to come together as church leaders, of all people groups and talk openly, honestly and transparently about this great challenge to the church. I was personally, pleased after a ministry trip to Holland; a wonderful "white" fellow pastor and myself shared our experiences and hope for the unity of the church. What encouraged me was here was a white minister, sharing his struggle to shed the feeling of superiority gained from the invisible benefit of white privilege. We spoke for hours and I could feel his honesty. I was grateful he was willing to be vulnerable, because, that is the beginning of true love. I also experienced this while on a trip to London. A wonderful white minister in Christ was so excited to share with me his challenging upbringing, and how, his father reinforced racist sentiments in the home. He shared how coming to Christ, had an indelible impact on his view of the wrongness of his upbringing. I had the same encounter with a Spanish Minister in London who was so fervent about not regarding our ethnic differences. He backed up his words, as his lead pastor is of African descent (Black). These kinds of conversations are paramount to the success of future revival. In an authentic kind of way, the words of Martin Luther King Jr. seem to lead the way even for those of us in the church, "that a man will not be judged by the colour of his skin, but by the content of his character"; that remains a dream worth fighting for. Nevertheless, in a greater sense, Jesus has cast a vision for this reality for his church almost 2000 years ago in his death on the cross and resurrection from the grave.

church around "race" seems to pacify the real deep-seated issues, and we focus on the surface platform of "racial reconciliation". If Zetzer is correct, most, if not all, White Christians will need to undergo the second order change she mentioned. We shouldn't ignore the inevitable challenges that will come with these changes; largely because a great deal of power will need to be relinquished for this dialogue to happen.

Sadly, in my many years of ministerial experience, I have seen firsthand the debilitating consequences of the persistence of white privilege. For example, many so-called international groups (groups that have ministry extending worldwide) are 100% led by whites in America, even when some of the largest churches among those groups are outside of America and among non-White constituents. There are also ministries that have evangelism strategies labeled "Black Evangelism" or "Hispanic Evangelism". Isn't that interesting? I don't know of any predominantly Black or Hispanic group labeling ministries "White Evangelism". Forgive me if this seems divisive, this is not the intent – just my real world experience with the subtlety and persistence of white privilege.[84]

The church has a long way to go to truly demonstrate the spirit of Jesus Christ in the earth. I know this may sound simplistic but I often wonder what the Kingdom of Heaven will be like. Is it going to be a reflection of what we have here on earth, or is it going to be a more endearing reality? Will there be different areas in the kingdom for specific cultural groups to congregate and worship God? What kind of practice or preparation are we making here now? Whites worship with Whites, Blacks with Blacks,

---

[84] I was talking to a friend of my mine (white female) who attends a church in California. As we discussed the dynamics of multi-culturalism in the church, she was happy to tell me that her church of some 3000 members had a very diverse mix of races. I asked about the composition of the leadership – was the pastor white or black? She sent me the churches website; under the drop down tab of the leadership team were pictures of 7 or 8 anglo-christians. Not one other race made up the team. I pointed this out to her and she was shocked; not that she didn't know, but she just never realized it. This is white privilege exemplified.

Hispanic with Hispanic, Asian with Asian and so on and so on[85]. Yes, I know, language, music style, culture are all legitimate obstacles, and all add to the complexities of this proposal. But, are these all going to disappear in a moment at the appearing of Jesus? Will the black Christian lose her blackness and the white Christian lose his whiteness? I recall Jesus sending the apostles to people of other cultures, languages, and certainly, this includes different musical styles and genres.

The Church must face this challenge and see the Great Commission for what it really is – an enormous challenge to the fabric of our Christian reality. I am honestly frustrated with the limitations of my personal socio-cultural, and economic Christian environment, our evident lack of zeal for the Great Commission. It makes me feel small in God's economy. I am not suggesting that the process of change will be easy. A paradigm shift does not happen overnight. However, I am challenging us- Black, White, Asian, Hispanic, Arabs, Persian, and Native Indian, to commit ourselves to the work of the Great Commission, irrespective of where we must go. I believe God will and does call Hispanic to evangelize non-Hispanics, and Blacks to evangelize non-Blacks etc. The church must see herself far greater and more powerful than any socio-political and historical tradition, for the execution of the Great Commission. Sometimes I feel so ashamed of the church because we fail to rise above the socio-political drama of the world, we fail to exemplify a true "oneness" church - a church that celebrates all people, irrespective of ethnicity, or nationalities, and which seeks genuine fellowship among all saints.

---

[85] Most Christians become exasperated when this topic is discussed. We seems not to want to deal with it. Its hard work; it calls for a tremendous amount of honest, open dialogue that frankly, most are afraid to have. It is easier for us to turn this topic into a racial maze, and bury our heads in the proverbial sand. Whites think, blacks are being aggravating, blacks think, whites are dishonest and patronizing. Seriously, let's honestly answer the question. How will the Kingdom solve this problem? Do we have a role to play in that process now? My hope is that there will be a group of spirit filled men and women from all backgrounds who will come together and work towards the realization of what Jesus has done and what Paul taught, the middle wall has been broken down.

In the last chapter, I stated that the commission of the Gospel was given to the twelve; it bears repeating again, because the Great Commission carries the same weight of responsibility for us in the 21st century. Just as the apostles were sent to lands unknown, and contended with language barriers, culture differences and, religious resistance, we must commit ourselves to do the same. We must possess a drive to accomplish the vision, to fill the earth with the good news of Christ's Lordship and gift of salvation. We cannot separate this from Christianity; to be Christian is to be inextricably tied to the assignment of the Great Commission. The early church was obsessive about worship, fellowship, sound doctrine, and reaching more and more people with the good news. I appreciate the complexity of the many issues facing us, but I believe Jesus has given to his church a powerful authority to break down every stronghold that exist, that attempts to paralyze the church.

I close this chapter with a stern warning to the church. In the first epistle of Peter chapter 4:17-18, Peter instructs that a time is coming when judgment would begin in the house of God. God is going to clean up His church, He will return for a bride that is without spot or wrinkle. There is no place in the church of Jesus Christ for prevailing sinful spirits, attitudes and practices of ethnic division and hate. This is a maniacal monster in the church, a very destructive force. I don't believe God will leave this spirit in the church unchecked. He will judge it! We shouldn't be challenged with the fact that these attitudes and practices exist; from the Fall, sin entered the world and will be present until the end. These attitudes and practices are manifestations of sin, what saddens me is their persistence and acceptance by many who claim to be in the Body of Christ. Some demonstrate destructive ethnic and cultural sentiments with arrogant mindsets and attitudes; others allow it by their passivity. I have many friends who are in organizations that have blatant practices and systems that promotes one people group over another, but act as if it doesn't exist; they sit passively by and allow it to continue.

Can anyone really hold racist beliefs and be saved, and go to heaven? I think not! Do not confuse these attitudes and beliefs about different people groups, what is commonly called "racism", with prejudice[86]. Peter himself allowed a prejudice spirit to impact him, but he learned his lesson (Acts 10) and changed. We too must learn our lesson. The church has done little to address these core issues addressed in this chapter. I believe the Lord will hold us accountable, and judge our indifference and unwillingness to deal with these issues head on. I mentioned earlier that I wasn't prescribing programs in this book, but allow me this one recommendation. I f we are going to deal honestly with the execution of the Great Commission, it will call for leaders of every group – White, Black, Hispanic, Asian, Middle Eastern, Native Indian, etc., to courageously sit together and discuss the issues raised in this book, particularly in this section. I do believe God has people who are sensing, in a real way, the universality of the church and who understand the need to come together, across ethnic lines, assembling together to celebrate Jesus, to demonstrate a true oneness in Christ.

---

[86] It is important that we understand the difference between racism and prejudice. Racism is the belief that all members of each race possess characteristics or abilities specific to that race, especially to distinguish it as inferior or superior to another race or races. Prejudice; however is preconceived opinion that is not based on reason or actual experience. Prejudice, prevails in many quarters both biblically and in modern times, but we are hard pressed to fine racism in the scriptures. As I stated earlier, the ethnic and cultural challenges found in scripture is based on religious difference than on deep seeded racist ideas.

CHAPTER 10

Blacks and the Mission Endeavour

A few months ago, I began reading about the role that African-Americans (Blacks) played in the mission endeavour. On one hand, I was pleasantly surprised, but on the other, disappointed. As I read an article by David Cornelius[87], *A Historical Survey of African Americans in World Missions,* I couldn't help but feel a sense of deep disappointment, and, I admit, anger. Colonialism and imperialism have had such a devastating impact on the Black faith community. Those who attempted to obey the Great Commission were Black preachers who, i) stayed at home [on the plantation, the region or community once the bastion of the slave industry] to preach to other blacks, ii) made their way back to Africa to evangelize other blacks; or iii) made their way to the Caribbean to preach to slaves and ex-slaves. Even in recent history, the church organization that I belong to, after 60 years of international ministry, still primarily evangelizes ex-pats from the Caribbean who migrate to Europe [Great Britain] and North America. The few attempts made at expanding the work into non- Black countries have gone unnoticed and unrecognized. Pioneered churches are in India, one of the greatest unreached harvest fields in the world, but there is very little effort to capitalize on this tremendous ministry opportunity.

---

[87] David Cornelius makes a good attempt at identifying the issues facing the so-called Black church. I agree with him 100% when he notes that "the African American church is a sleeping giant in the area of international missions: a giant that is being awakened by her Lord. Only God knows the extent to which His Kingdom will be strengthened as the full potential of this giant is realized in international missions!

It seems like the damage is irreparable, the devil has won the victory. But, I still believe God for a mighty move of His spirit and a great end time revival.

If I focus primarily on the implication of the historical elements of this issue, we may miss the real point. The historical element is necessary for contextualizing where we have been, but its purpose is best served if it instructs us, and we never allow somethings to be repeated. We must learn from history and challenge the social and cultural constructs that have developed. There must be brave young men and women who, under the guidance and vigor of the Holy Spirit, will transmit this Gospel of the Kingdom to regions beyond their own cultural and ethnic ethos. This calls for radical and revolutionary obedience to the Great Commission. It calls for men that will hazard their lives[88] for the cause of the kingdom; women, who will surrender all for the glorious triumph of a people born unto God; and couples that will brave the uncharted regions of the world looking for a people that do not know God. It's also a call for churches to commission missionaries with outlandish and imprudent assignments to save those who are lost; for Christian businesspeople to allocate thousands, even millions of dollars to the work of the mission field (be it next door or around the world); for educators to give up their summer breaks to teach in some remote region on the planet; and for health practitioners to surrender high wages for an AIDs ravaged corner in Africa or diseased and impoverished slum in Mexico.

Should any of this be affected by the colour of one's skin? By human standards, maybe, but by God's standard, never. The Great Commission is not given to special groups of elite people who, because of economic stability, can send money to the mission field[89]. It is a collective endeavour, by all those who have come into the glorious truth of Jesus Christ. It is a call for all to incarnate themselves among people who are in need of God.

---

[88] Acts 15:26

[89] Do not miss the point here. God is sovereign, and He expects those who through his grace have been afford the privilege of much possessions to utilize those resources for the establishment of the Kingdom of God. To whom much is given, much is required (Luke 12:48). What should not happen, is that those who are endowed with much resources, misunderstand there true status.

My prayer is that, in the next few years, there will be an impetus of resilient people, who refuse to accept any limitation in the execution of the Great Commission. A young man in Jamaica will feel the call to a South American city to plant an indigenous church there. An African woman will hear God calling her to a remote village in Australia to work with homeless children; an El Salvadorian man will feel a deep burden for the Polish people. A Jewish boy will hear God calling him to pastor a church in Germany. The people of God will break free from all the limitations of human capacity and champion the great cause of the Kingdom.

This is the emergent Apostolic church at her best. She thrives, where there is little finance, "silver and gold have I none, but such as I have give I you"[90]. She refuses to keep silent, even at the threat of death, "...did we not straightly command that you should not teach in this name...and behold you have filled Jerusalem with your doctrine..."[91]. She plants churches by unnamed saints; she commissions people for the work of the ministry. She is less interested in organizational institutionalization, and more interested in organic multiplication with a spontaneous impulse. She is a movement, not an organization. She cannot be stopped, or controlled. She is impossible to figure out. We find her exploding in war torn regions, expanding in AIDs infested villages. She penetrates prison facilities, affecting hardened criminals with life transforming power. She invades academia; sits on the bench in the courtroom, presides over multi-national corporate meetings. She is found consoling men and women ravished by a life of same sex relationships. She spends long nights walking the streets with ladies of the night. She is an unstoppable force, she is found in the spirit of just men and women made perfect by the blood of the lamb.

---

[90] Acts 3:6

[91] Acts 5:28

SECTION IV

Apostolic Inheritance

CHAPTER 11

Re-discovering an Apostolic Inheritance

I was in a conference a few years back entitled *Re-Discovering our Apostolic Inheritance*. It was a good conference but I think one essential aspect eluded us in the dialogue. This is largely because we usually hyper-spiritualize deep-rooted problems, problems that are deeper than the outward symptoms we experience. One speaker spoke on "why we need to re-discover…" and with expert precision, explained what it was that we have lost. It re-affirmed essential doctrines, but unfortunately, I think the speaker fell short of the real problem.

The deep-rooted problem is akin to someone who has a serious illness but is unaware of the generational predisposition in his or her bloodline. I remember when we were having our second child, during a routine ultrasound the doctors saw something concerning on the babies hand. With great concern, we were booked for an appointment with a geneticist. We walked into the office completely unaware of why we were there. As the doctor began asking questions, we answered hesitantly, not wanting to find out anything tragic. The doctor explained to us what they saw could be because of an extra chromosome and what that could mean. After several more questions, we arrived at the cause of the issue. Although I was aware that I had an extra digit (an extra digit is an additional finger without bone, properly called polydactyly) as a child, I was oblivious that I could pass it on to my children. The doctor asked if either of us ever had extra digits. With a sense of nostalgia, I nonchalantly and innocently explained that my mother, my eldest sister and I had them. The crisis was over. Polydactyly is a genetic trait that has a 50% chance of being passed on. Of my eight children, five have had polydactyly.

So, here we are as a church trying to find out what has gone wrong. However, most of us are completely unaware of the depth of the problem. The problem is not that people don't love God; nor is it that they have totally lost their values. It is not that Satan is so crafty that he has caused many to lose their way, (although some have); the problem is not even found in the Bible per se. The real problem is to be found in our development processes. By this I mean our methods of operation, how we have structured our churches. It is our negligence to hold steadfastly to a method of doing the work of God as prescribed in the New Testament. I want to be careful not to bite the hand that has fed me; I acknowledge that I came into a church that was operating and functioning well enough to provide a place for me to come and be discipled. Nevertheless, the reality is that God likely winked at how we did His work and allowed it to prosper. Years later, in many quarters in the Western Hemisphere, we now find ourselves seeking to re-discover what defines us, who we are supposed to be.

Jesus said, "Upon this rock I build my church and the gates of hell shall not prevail against it". What we must ask is how was He building it? As discussed earlier, the New Testament teaches that the church was built on the apostles and prophets, with Jesus as the chief corner stone. Can we then seek to know what has been lost without an investigation of this vital element of Kingdom ministry? To understand the real problem we need to understand church history. We must look at two areas of religious or church history to get the right picture. First, we must understand the ecclesiastical history of the early church, the first 300 years of Apostolic ministry. Then, we must study the period from the beginning of Constantine rule[92], until our present day. In these two periods of church history, you will find two completely different methods of operation. One is from heaven and therefore divine; the other is from earth, therefore carnal and natural.

---

[92] On February 313, Constantine met with Licinius in Milan and formulated the Edict of Milan, which granted religious tolerance and freedom for all to follow their faith without oppression. Not only were they free but seized property was returned.

Let's look at some key features of the early church and make some comparison with our present day church experiences.

The Early Church:

- Had no building (by necessity) to worship in, but experienced explosive growth (lack of building didn't hinder the movement at all, if anything it actually inspired further expansion)
- Many of the leaders had limited technology but remained progressive.
- Had very little hierarchical structure but the church advanced.

On the other hand, the church in **The Constantinian era** (300+):

- Had large sacred buildings (great focus on the building as the place where people would come to meet God)
- The elders became "clergy" and professional, separated from the people, and employed new techniques to further the cause.

Now, which of the two eras are we modeled after? If you said the Constantine era you would be correct. Let's go a little further to see how this form of Christendom has impacted Apostolic ministry and history.

- The Constantine mode of church engaged in an attractional method that centralized the church in relation to its surrounding. In other words, the church building became the central place that people gathered once they were Christianized. The focus was on the "come and see" aspect of ministry.
- This era focused its attention on dedicated, sacred building/places of worship. The building became the "church" and completely altered how we perceived ourselves as *the church*. With this schematic the people of God organized in one static and institutionalized form. Apostolic Mission died, and was replaced with the seeds of

Catholic missiological strategy that transferred the teaching and doctrine of this new church system[93].

- Leadership shifted into one institutionally organized professional clergy, operating primarily in a Pastor-Teacher mode. The church was separated into two groups, clergy and lay people; this was **unheard of in the New Testament.** (Don't misunderstand this point, the early church was very diligent about leadership, but what they had was very different from what we experience in our churches today). To be a leader in the first century meant join the line for martyrdom; leaders were killed first, hence, Paul had to encourage men not to avoid the office of a Bishop. Today, we are beginning to see bishops who are self-appointed, who have no church or souls to oversee, and who are primarily in the office for status and economic gain and entitlement.

- Constantine's institutionalization offered grace in the form of sacraments administered by a professional authority called the priesthood. Only clergy could preside over the Lord's Table, do baptisms, bless babies etc.

Now, I know there are those who will say that what we do is not from the Constantinian Era but from the Old Testament model of priesthood. That would be unfortunate, because Hebrews tells us that we are no longer under that order. The priesthood changed, from Levi to Judah (at least for the church). We must follow the early apostles, who followed the new order of priesthood. More could be said about this but is beyond the scope of this book.

---

[93] I don't believe the church in the Constantinian era was the church God was building. This was a false religious system led by human government. All the New Testament writers speak of men who were imposers to the real faith of Jesus Christ. What religious history has failed to do is distinguish between the two eras, between the false and the real church. Once the Constantinian era took front stage, the true church of the apostles went underground. She has existed in many places, forms, and by different names over the centuries but has never lost her primitive spirit and zeal for the mission. Today, she has surfaced and joined the mainstream because of religious freedoms not afforded before. It is this church of which I speak.

In view of the early church, we see that:

- The early church was extremely missional (on mission) in mode and theology. The church invaded its surroundings, planted churches everywhere, and raised up leaders. The early church was a "going, sending" organism. The *"come and see"* element followed a *"go and tell"* attitude and practice.
- With no secured spaces outside of their homes, the early church grew exponentially. How did God locate 3000 men [not including the women and children] after the revival at Pentecost? The early church had no buildings for the first 300+ years, yet she grew rapidly. The Pentecostal revival was strategic and reflected the missional methodology of God. Seventeen nations were represented, the Holy Ghost descended and in a few days the experience and the message of Pentecost would be spread throughout the entire Roman Empire and beyond.
- The leadership in the early church was Apostolic and dynamic. There was one class of believers, building the church through gifts and offices. The fivefold ministry was the active principal for leadership. In Acts 13, we hear nothing of a single office Pastor, but rather of Prophets and Teachers, five in total, who were the principle leaders in that great missionary sending, Great Commission church in Antioch. The early Apostles knew their role and were not willing to compromise it. In Acts 6, when conflict began to rise in the church, the Apostles didn't take on the pastoral duties to manage the daily administration of the distribution of food, instead they called the church together and had them appoint men to supervise in that area.
- With house churches all over, covenant believers enacted the communion in many places at many times. This is consistent with the Jewish practice of the *Sadar* that is enacted in every home by the priest of the home, the father or male head.

As I reflect on the state of the church and its need to reclaim vital elements of church life and ministry, it is clear that, unless we are able to shed the baggage of a man made system for church ministry, we will continue to lose our influences in our culture[94]. Many churches feel comfortable with their position and method of ministry, largely because we have cut ourselves off from much of our cultural realities. Our separation is so complete that we no longer understand what it takes to reach people. Our marriage to the attractional model of ministry has blinded us to the fact that the world is not coming to us. We are a far cry from the early church government the apostles set up. We have inherited a system that is pagan in its roots and faulty, at best, to bring redemption to mankind the way a true apostolic system can.

Somehow we didn't hear the believers when they were crying *"we need to get out from the four walls"*, and now we have convinced ourselves that we are doing fine. We missed the point that there are more people outside the church than there are in the church! We can hide from the world, shouting platitudes from the pulpit about no prayer in schools, homosexuality on the rise, no God in society, all while the cure for these social and spiritual ills are in our possession – the message of Jesus Christ, carried by believers into every corner of society.

We have lost the innate, genetic Apostolic spirit that governs church leadership, culture, mindset, and attitude. We lost the motivation for adventure, to take risks, to defy danger, possess a sort of wildness[95] that intimidates people, inherent in all children born of faith. Now we talk but do very little. We must re-evaluate our systems of operation because in them are the seeds of an apostolic genius [I am not talking about a single person] waiting to unfold. We must regain the ancient system that propelled the church into new uncharted territories, released those with the zeal for revival, challenged the superstructure of the Roman Empire, reached into the very courts of Caesar, and possessed servants of Rome with the Gospel of Jesus Christ. The church is dynamic, daring, brave,

---

[94] This is one of the main points of this book; our method of operation has affected our ability to affect the world around us. Attractionalism is not an apostolic methodology. Faced with a growing secular society, antagonistic to Christianity the church must return to her primitive apostolic roots:, an apostolic incarnational missiology. Interesting enough all those, words carry the ideas of "going" in them.

[95] Many characters in the Bible were characterized like this. John the Baptist was among them. These men did not possess social dignities, were not refined, learned men; their characteristics and personalities where brazen, sharp, and thunderous.

refusing to be inoculated with the tranquilizing drug of tolerance and consumerism – the new gods of the age. Re-structuring the church to her former state will change our assumptions about people and their service to God, and challenge leaders to face the world with a new attitude for Kingdom realization. We must turn our backs on the state-church system we have inherited. Constantine is the father of the state-church. Christian Sabbath keepers have attributed the change from Saturday worship to Sunday worship to him. I am afraid that, although fundamentally incorrect, he has given the modern church much more than just a calendar change. Most of what takes place in our churches is a direct result of his system. He was never baptized; water was sprinkled on his forehead by a cleric on his deathbed. Unfortunately, we in the 21st century have for the most part accepted, lock, stock, and barrel the form of church ministry and governance developed in his era.

CHAPTER 12

Conclusion: Call to Action

I believe I would be accurate in assuming that a large number of the churches and church leaders that read this will conclude that my findings and statements, while rational, may not be practical or applicable. I agree *if* you are from the school that is satisfied with the status quo and hold to a perspective that these suggestions are not possible because, as church leaders, you are satisfied with your current paradigm. Unfortunately, that paradigm is Contstantianism, and not Apostolic. What is interesting is that there are now groups who do not shared an orthodox theology of God, who are espousing the idea of apostolicity as a defining attribute of their church ministry practice.

This book was written with one intention, to challenge the church, and leadership particularly, to return the church to an authentic apostolic model. I am calling churches to a stronger Great Commission focus. Churches, who are now experiencing a measure of ecclesiastical success, must think about the possibilities if they return to an ancient apostolic mode of operation. Maybe we need to rethink our ideas of success. Leonard Sweet notes in his book, *"Summoned to Lead"*, *"*... nothing fails like success; it freezes you in patterns that brought you success 12 months ago but that will bring you failure today. Most churches are operating with information about how things were years ago".[96]

The call to action is for us to re-evaluate how we have been building the church. At the forefront will be our ability to look back and remodel the church the way I believe God intended it to be. Let us strip away the structure and institutionalization of the church and return to an organic, metabolic, reproducing church. Let's stop putting so much emphasis into ministry facilities and then turn them into little monasteries where people come and meet God. We have operated for too long on the "come and see" aspect to the Gospel. The kingdom needs a "go and tell" kind of people who will answer the call, to go and gather the people and bring them to "come and see".

Can we truly be apostolic and not have an incarnational attitude to the work of the ministry? Yes, we need buildings; there must be places to gather. No debate there. But, much of our ministries have centered our existence on the beauty, grandeur and location of our structures. The building should serve as a tool to effectively train and send out workers into the mission field, locally, regionally, nationally and internationally. It serves as a place to care for, equip and celebrate our life shared in Christ.

The church is a launching pad from which we strategically devise plans to reach the world. I think it is foolish for churches to exist for an entire generation and not plant another church, not send out workers to start pioneered works. Every leader should have his/her sights on planting another church within the life time of that ministry; if not directly, at least indirectly through partnering with other churches, sowing finances into starting churches, sending workers to aid in church planting projects and so on.

---

[96] Leonard Sweet, *Summoned to Lead*, (Grand Rapids, Michigan, Zondervan, 2004, pg. 166) Grand Rapids, Michigan. I have noticed that so many of our churches live in nostalgia. I have even heard young people say things like "we need to get back to the old days ". So many of our churches/ministries are frozen in time, unwilling to change, adapt, be flexible, and make needed adjustments that will move the ministry forward. Yesterday's successes threaten to blind us from the needed actions that will bring success today. What was done in yester years, even as recent as two decades ago, does not bring success today.

I pray that there is someone reading this that feels something in your gut, in your spirit, saying that you are to be involved in church planting. Pray and seek the face of God to open doors for you. Either you will give your life to a church plant or maybe just your finances, or you may only participate in projects throughout the course of your life e.g. short term missions. I hope you are part of a church that has church expansion and planting as a major agenda in its vision and mission statements, but more important, in its actions. I hope some young person reading this is stirred to give their life to the work of the Gospel as a missionary. Someone who actually sees the kingdom's demand for labourers, willing to leave the comfort of home and go into the world on mission for God. Maybe you are called to the market place, business, education, politics, social service. Maybe you are called to the foreign field, maybe to a home mission work. Whatever the call, wherever the call, I pray that the fire of God will swell in your spirit and give you the desire to give everything up for Christ's sake.

This call to action is inviting us to strip away the ideas of the clergy and laity, a culture of an elite priesthood of know-it-alls, and restore the biblically based fivefold ministry Paul taught in Ephesians 4. We must return to a biblical model for leadership in the church. Leadership is not based in titles as much as it is based in "calling" and "gifting". God places people in the body to accomplish his work and he gives them the ability to do that work. There is no doubt that there are those who are called to official offices that require strong administrative skills. However, I have researched and have not found the clergy-laity system/ structure we have adapted in scripture. The church has fallen so far from the model Jesus gave that we have adapted ungodly practices and sanctified them. The late Bishop M. R. Saunders Sr. once said, if we sanctify immorality we will never get it out of the church. Although we are not talking about morality here, the point is applicable. Anytime you sanctify something that God never intended to be sanctified, you give that thing life and cannot remove it from your influence without drastic measures.

Some of you may take offense to this, (I hope not), but the clergy-laity model has caused such disparity between the people of God that some lord over God's heritage. The clergy has become like gods over the people. This has given rise to a strange episcopacy among many groups. There are many other books you can read for a deeper examination of this subject but, for clarity and understanding here, we are contending for an *Apostolic* model of leadership not a "catholic" model, from which these concepts emanate.

I know that for the more established churches this proposal seems almost impossible. There would be too much to deal with in dismantling the current structures. It's too much work to steer the minds of the people back to a true biblical model, for many church goers have become comfortable with the "clergy" doing the bulk of the work[97]. To change that now would mean that the saints would have to start giving themselves in ways they have never done before.

My final call to action is for leaders, or anyone reading this book, to pull out a map of the world and begin to pray about where in the world God can use your influence. It may be too easy to say "I just have to look around to see an enormous amount of needs, why bother look for somewhere else"? Or, "I am just going to work in my local home town" None of these statements are wrong, but we must remember that the earth is the Lord's, He can and will send workers anywhere He chooses. Pray that your church will begin to see the World as its mission field. Pray that your church will develop or enhance its missions budget. You give specifically to the work of the mission field. There are places in the world where apostolic missionaries are struggling to expand the work of the Gospel because of lack of resources;[98] your dollar may double in some places. Finally, pray

---

[97] In a Bible class we discussed how evangelism happens, one of the saints made a startling statement that confirmed how most believers think. They stated that they always thought the pastor was the expert and if we, the saints, can get people to the church, the expert would get them saved. How faulty is that thinking? This corporate thought process is a major disability to the growth of the church. The pastor is not the expert on growing the church. If he is an expert at anything, it should be on the care of people, and even this job is not conducted in isolation to others.

[98] We have experienced time challenges, our local church wasn't able to continue support for one of our missionaries on the global field, so she had to come home.

for workers to be sent into the field[99]. Pray for church planters and church planting families. Pray for your pastor(s), church leaders, that they will follow a true apostolic vision for the church. Then we will see the emergent Apostolic church at her best.

---

[99] We are pleased as our church since its first plant has now commissioned a retired couple to the Island of Grenada to plant churches in the Island. This recent commissioning is exactly what we are talking about here, this missionary couple purposed to give their retirement years to the service of God. With no small vision the idea is to reach an entire Island with the apostolic message of the cross.

Afterward

Let's be real about what we are doing. The work of the church is serious business and with the little time we have left, let us make a good go at it. Jesus taught his disciples, "upon this Rock, I will build My church". This statement should make it clear the church belongs to Him. Our culture is preoccupied with the need for importance. I am sure you have seen in church foyers, pictures of that assemble's "founder". Really!? Founder? Why don't we use words that speak more of what the person really did, *plant*. It is more accurate to describe the planting of a church by a missionary pastor as the person God used to initiate that work in His vineyard. The term "founder" completely misleads as to who "started" the church. Jesus clearly stated that the church is "His"; "I will build 'my' church", is very direct.

The foremost quality that must govern ministry effectiveness is a clear understanding of who we are, in relation to God and who He is, in the Church enterprise. Be mindful and diligent to keep Jesus at the center of the "business" of church ministry. Remember, you and I are like grass or the flower that fades away, here today, gone tomorrow. No matter what you are doing, someone else is going to come and take over from you. We're not islands, we work as members on a larger team – your spouse if you're married, your church staff if you are a local church leader or ministry director; and all of us have the assistance of the angelic host as *paraklets*, helpers who come along side to help us in times of need.

Allow me to invite you into the *"mystery of ministry"*. Are you weary of the same old practice of "church"? How about something more daring, adventurous, dangerous? I can say, with a great deal of confidence, that many in the church world have surrendered to life in a bubble; a safe place where we are inoculated from the dangers of a world infested with spiritual decay, death, disease, pain, hurt and confusion. In an effort to avoid contamination, we recluse to our monastery called "church". Here we can sing and preach about how ugly the world system is, how sinful people have become, and defend against all forms of compromise.

The other extreme is that some think the solution to effective ministry in a sinful world is to become clones of it; to resemble the worlds system, and in the process, we actually assume essential qualities of the thing we are replicating. Now we can't tell who's who. Christians are lumped into the same group as everyone else without any particular distinction about them. Contrary to popular belief, the mystery I speak of contains the belief that it is possible to be distinct, while being touchable, reachable, and relatable to the lost, those without Christ. How is it that Christ, being God in the flesh, was able to interact with people in every lifestyle and never lose his God-ness? That is the very heart of the mystery of the ministry. The incarnation is the experience where the eternal God humbled himself and became obedient unto death and came to people like you and I, people in low degree, sinners. Yet, he was without sin. How do we do this? How do we pattern this act of the incarnation?

If you are a church leader, think about adapting an AIM framework™[100] into your philosophy of ministry. As I stated before, I do not care to recommend direct strategies for you to implement into your ministry. I sincerely believe that no two churches are the same, it is therefore, very difficult to guarantee that what works in one context will work in another. However, there are principles and processes that can inform how and what we do. Ask yourself the following questions:

- How **apostolic** is your ministry? I'm not asking you to stand on a doctrinal soapbox celebrating what you believe. I am however, asking you to think deeply about how your understanding of doctrine shapes what your ministry believes and practices.
- To what degree does your church/ministry, and you as an individual, exercise incarnationalism as a vital act of ministry?
- Lastly, to what degree have you and/or your church, dealt with the divisive attitudes and practices due to the cultural and ethnic differences among people groups (racism), cross- cultural ministry

---

[100] At the time of the writing of this book, we are completing the ministry resource and workshop entitled "Developing an AIM Framework: How to Fulfill Your Ministries Inherent Missional DNA". For information, how a workshop can be arranged see our contact information at the back of the book.

and the Great Commission beyond your primary cultural group? How committed are you to the missional mandate of the church. (You may only need answer this question if you are interested in a global response to the gospel in your church/ministry. If you are settled with a nationalistic strategy move on.)

If you are willing to wrestle and reflect with these few questions, you may be ready for true spiritual and ministerial transformation.

About the Author

Alan Todd was born in Toronto, Canada to Jamaican parents. He has served in ministry for 26 years and has a burden for people globally. He was called to the ministry shortly after accepting Christ in his late teens. He is a gifted and sought after conference speaker, seminar and workshop facilitator. He has studied at Tyndale University, Royal Roads University, and Canada Christian College in Religious Studies, Leadership, and Church Ministry. He shares in ministry with a team of dedicated men and women. He is the lead pastor-teacher in his local church capacity, and continues to minister as an evangelist, strengthening the body of Christ internationally. He has ministered in Scandanavia, Central Europe, and the Caribbean and across North America. He is the Principle of Kingdom Expansion, a ministry he founded in 2006, preaching and teaching the expansion of the Kingdom of God. As a denominational leader, he sits as the National Administrator on the Executive Board of Bethlehem United Churches of Jesus Christ (Apostolic) – Canada. He provides oversight to a church plant in Grenada, W.I. and continues to do missions work in St. Vincent and the Grenadines. He is committed to developing his work in the area of an *AIM framework*, a workshop designed to assist churches, particularly new church plants, embed a missional DNA in their development of ministry.

Alan and his wife of 20 years, Allison, have eight children and are homeschoolers. Alan loves the outdoors, horseback riding and can sometimes be found bungee jumping. He boasts that his next feat will be skydiving. Stay tuned!

To Book an Engagement for Alan to Speak at your event contact:

www.visitalantodd.com
alantodd@visitalantodd.com
tcmf@visitalantodd.com

Reference List

Bacon, F. *Essays*. New York: Cosimo Classics, 2007.

Barna G. and Jackson H., *High Impact African-American Churches*, Regal Books, 2004 pg. 115

C. Johnson and P. Smith, *Africans in America,* WGBN Educational Foundations, 1998, page 292

Csorba, Les. *Trust: the one thing that makes or breaks a leader.* Thomas Nelson Press, 2004. Chapter 8: "The Affair" pages 134-145.

Eldridge, John. *The Heart: Waking the Dead,* Thomas Nelson Press, 2007. Nashville Tennessee

Heward-Mills, Dag. *Church Planting*, Parchment House, Accra Ghana, 2004

Morinis, Alan. *Everyday Holiness: The Jewish Spiritual Path of Mussar.* Boston, Massachusetts Trumpeter Books, 2007

Ritzer, G. *The McDonaldization of Society.* Los Angeles: Sage, 1993, 2013.

W. E. B. Du Bois, *Black Reconstruction in America, 1860-1880* (New York: Free Press, 1995 reissue of 1935 original), pp. 700-701.

Swanson, K., *Apostate: The Men who Destroyed the Christian West.* Colorado, Generations with Vision, 2013

Zetzer, H.A. (2005). *White Out: Privilege and Its Problems.* In S.K. Anderson & V.A. Middleton (eds.), Explorations in Privilege, Oppression, and Diversity (pp. 5). Belmont, CA: Thomson Brooks/Cole.

Web based References

http://www.elyrics.net/read/h/hannah-montana-lyrics/the-climb-lyrics.
html n.d

www.apologeticsindex.org/2222-worship-of-angels

Fausset's Bible Dictionary, Electronic Database Copyright (c)1998 by
Biblesoft

http://www.selfmasterysecrets.com/success/what-napoleon-hill-and-
andrew-carnegie-taught-me-about-opportunity/.

http://www.brainyquote.com/quotes/quotes/h/henrywadsw129800.html

www.medicinet.com/miscarriage/article.html

www.awcf.org

http://www.washingtonpost.com/wp-dyn/articles/A8427-2005Mar28.
html

Article: The Marxist Roots of Black Liberation Theology http://www.acton.
org/pub/commentary/2008/04/02/marxist-roots-black-liberation-theology

http://www.webtruth.org/articles/church-issues-30/the-purpose-driven-
church-(a-critique)-59.html

Index

W

CPSIA information can be obtained at www.ICGtesting.com
Printed in the USA
BVOW02s1455140615

404462BV00001B/4/P